Output Measures for Public Libraries

A Manual of Standardized Procedures

Second edition

Prepared for the Public Library Development Program

by
Nancy A. Van House
Mary Jo Lynch
Charles R. McClure
Douglas L. Zweizig
Eleanor Jo Rodger

American Library Association
Chicago and London

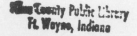
Cover designed by Thomas Sollers

Text designed by Deborah Doering

Composed by Impressions, Inc. in
ITC Garamond and Gill Sans on
a Penta-driven Autologic APS-μ5
Phototypesetting system.

Printed on 50-pound Glatfelter, a
pH-neutral stock, and bound in
10-point Carolina cover stock by
Malloy Lithographing, Inc.

Library of Congress Cataloging-in-Publication Data

Output measures for public libraries.

   Rev. ed. of: Output measures for public libraries /
Douglas Zweizig. 1982.
   Includes index.
   1. Public libraries—Evaluation—Handbooks, manuals,
etc. 2. Library statistics—Handbooks, manuals, etc.
I. Van House, Nancy A. II. Public Library Association.
New Standards Task Force. III. Zweizig, Douglas. Output
measures for public libraries.
Z678.85.O89 1987   027.473   87-11479
ISBN 0-8389-3340-8

Contents

Figures

Presidents' Message

The Public Library Association exists to assist public librarians in giving better service to users of their libraries. In that continuing tradition, over the past four years a major project has come to fruition in the Public Library Development Program, of which this volume is one product.

Many librarians and libraries have contributed expertise, work, and money to this program. As presidents of the Public Library Association during the four years just past, we owe a special debt to the faithful hard work and professional excellence of the members of the New Standards Task Force and especially to the Task Force's guiding hand, its chair, Karen Krueger.

PLA is justifiably proud of the participation of so many of its members in an effort that promises so much to the improvement of public library service in the years to come. As presidents of PLA during the development of the program, we wish to express our appreciation to all who have been associated with it.

Nancy M. Bolt, President, 1983–84
Charles W. Robinson, President, 1984–85
Patrick M. O'Brien, President, 1985–86
Kathleen M. Balcom, President, 1986–87

Foreword

OUTPUT MEASURES FOR PUBLIC LIBRARIES, second edition, is one component of the Public Library Development Program (PLDP), a combination of activities and products developed by the Public Library Association to assist public libraries in the areas of planning, measurement, and evaluation. These activities and products were designed to continue the philosophy and work done previously by PLA in this area. PLDP was supported by the Public Library Association, the Chief Officers of State Library Agencies (COSLA), and the Urban Libraries Council (ULC). The three products developed as a part of the Public Library Development Program are:

Planning and Role Setting for Public Libraries by Charles R. McClure, Amy Owen, Douglas L. Zweizig, Mary Jo Lynch, and Nancy Van House (Chicago: American Library Association, 1987)

This manual, OUTPUT MEASURES FOR PUBLIC LIBRARIES, second edition

The design and specifications for a public library data service.

These tools are the result of discussions by the PLA New Standards Task Force regarding the need for new qualitative and quantitative standards for public libraries. Although some librarians prefer prescriptive quantitative standards, there was strong support at the 1984 ALA Conference Hearing for the position that library services should be tailored to specific communities and based on local planning and decision-making. The Task Force, having reviewed the enormous progress made by libraries and PLA in the areas of local planning and evaluation, decided to build on what had already been done rather than create national standards.

There were two primary building blocks for the Public Library Development Program, both of which were created largely due to the efforts of the PLA Goals, Guidelines, and Standards Committee. The first was *A Planning Process for Public Libraries* by Vernon E. Palmour et al. (Chicago: American Library Association, 1980). This step-by-step guide to local planning for public libraries was produced with support from a U.S. Office of Education grant. As a result of this publication and its use by libraries, it became apparent that libraries needed assistance with measuring their performance in terms of library services (outputs) rather than library resources (inputs). The second building block, *Output Measures for Public Libraries* by Douglas L. Zweizig and Eleanor Jo Rodger (Chicago: American Library Association, 1982), was developed to fill that need. *Output Measures* identified a set of measures related to common public library service activities and included a set of standardized procedures for these measures.

After a number of years of experience with these two tools, librarians were knowledgeable enough to articulate the strengths and weaknesses of both manuals. In addition, the Task Force identified two rather unexplored areas which seemed to have great potential for helping libraries choose directions and establish priorities. The first of these, the library roles concept, resulted from work done by Lowell Martin, who observed that public libraries try to do too much and as a result find it difficult to provide the quality of services desired. He suggested that the complex set of services public libraries provide their communities could be grouped under a set of service profiles, or roles, from which each library could choose a few on which to focus. Development of this roles concept was seen as an important element of a new or enhanced planning tool.

The second unexplored (or perhaps undeveloped) area is comparative data. In the measurement part of the planning process, librarians were looking at data on their library's performance and asking "compared to what?" Although internal comparison over time is preferred, the need for information on other libraries in similar communities with similar resources was real. The Task Force decided that the provision of such data in a timely manner would greatly enhance library planning efforts.

As a result of this review of libraries' planning and evaluation needs, the Public Library Development Program was created. The development of a revised planning manual with emphasis on role setting, the revision of the output measures manual, and the design of a data service that could provide libraries with comparative data for planning—all three closely interrelated—were seen by the Task Force as the best possible assistance PLA could give libraries. It was determined that prescriptive standards, if needed, should be developed at the state and local level.

With this idea and with funding for the project from COSLA, ULC, and individual public libraries, a contract was signed in 1985 with Charles R. McClure, president of Information Management Consultant Services Inc., for production of the desired tools. McClure, as principal investigator, and Mary Jo Lynch, Amy Owen, Nancy Van House, and Douglas Zweizig made up the project study team. In January 1987 they completed the planning and measurement manuals and the design and specifications for the public library data service.

The three products of the Public Library Development Program, described below, are designed to be used either together or independently.

- *Planning and Role Setting for Public Libraries* describes a step-by-step planning process and introduces the concept of role se-

lection. The manual guides the library as it reviews existing conditions and services, defines the library's mission, sets goals and objectives, chooses strategies for achieving objectives, and evaluates the results of the process.

- *Output Measures for Public Libraries,* second edition, describes a set of measures to assess common public library services. Instructions are included for collecting, analyzing, and interpreting data.

- The Public Library Data Service (PLDS) will collect and make accessible a selective set of data from public libraries across the country. It will contain four kinds of data:
  Selected output measures
  Library descriptors, including role choices
  Input data such as holdings, staff, and operating expenditures
  Community data such as population, age distribution, and income.

As this manual goes to press, the PLDS has been designed and is being tested. Implementation is scheduled for 1988.

The Public Library Development Program is both a continuation and a beginning. In order to assist public libraries in providing better library service in their communities, it has been necessary to look both at past experiences and future needs. There is no doubt the past has been exciting. With the progress of PLDP thus far, the future seems even more so.

PLA New Standards Task Force

Karen Krueger, chair
Carolyn Additon Anthony
Kathleen Mehaffey Balcom
Nancy M. Bolt
Mary Jo Detweiler
Ronald A. Dubberly
James H. Fish
June M. Garcia
Claudya B. Muller
Charles W. Robinson
Eleanor Jo Rodger
Elliot Shelkrot

Acknowledgments

Like the Constitution of the United States, this volume is the result of the work of many people. It is, of course, our hope it will engender the same kind of interest and discussion in the relatively small public library community as the Constitution did in the former colonies, but we make no claims to comparable literary excellence. We will be satisfied if this product and other products and services of the Public Library Development Program are useful to trustees, administrators, and staff members of public libraries.

The Public Library Association is grateful to many people and many institutions who have had a part in the Public Library Development Program during the past four years:

The Chief Officers of State Library Agencies and the Urban Library Council, co-sponsors with PLA of the Public Library Development Program. By their recognition and support of this effort, COSLA and ULC have provided the resource documents and services designed to assist public libraries in the provision of services to their users.

Nancy Bolt, who as President of PLA appointed the members of the New Standards Task Force and gave them their charge.

The New Standards Task Force (members listed below), whose professional experience, commitment, and ability to engage in endless hours of productive meetings gave shape, form, and guidance to the project.

Karen Krueger, who overfulfilled Nancy Bolt's expectations as the chair of the Task Force, and whose polite but firm leadership made sense from what often seemed confusion.

Charles Robinson, whose persistence in raising funds from public libraries all across the nation provided not only resources from but also participation by the public library community.

Gary Strong, the chair of COSLA, who provided the vision and leadership which elicited money, advice, and commitment from state libraries.

The over 150 individual public and state libraries (listed below) that contributed—and are still contributing—to the Public Library Development Program. Their commitment of funds has made the program and its products, of which this volume is one, truly a cooperative effort of America's public libraries.

Ronald Dubberly and Alex Ladenson, who for PLA and the Urban Libraries Council, respectively, provided administrative and financial management for the project.

The Study Team (listed below), whose patience, honesty, frankness, vision, and uncanny ability to meet unreasonable deadlines gave new meaning to the term "consultants."

ALA Publishing Services staff, notably Gary Facente and Helen Cline, for their continuing help and advice and their insistence on excellence in product design.

The Test Sites (listed below), without which reality might have been missed, and whose forebearance and suggestions have resulted in products more likely to be used and to improve public library service.

ELEANOR JO RODGER
Executive Director
Public Library Association

June 1987

New Standards Task Force

Appointed by PLA President Nancy Bolt in 1983, most NSTF members have changed their institutional affiliations in the meantime. Hence multiple credits appear after many names.

Chair: Karen J. Krueger (Arrowhead Library System, Wis.; Janesville, Wis., Public Library); *members:* Carolyn A. Anthony (Baltimore County and Skokie public libraries), Nancy Bolt (JNR Associates; Colorado State Library), Mary J. Detweiler (Prince William County, Md., Public Library; Dynix Inc.), Ronald A. Dubberly (Seattle and Atlanta-Fulton public libraries), June M. Garcia (Phoenix Public Library), Claudya B. Muller (Iowa State Library; Suffolk County, N.Y., Cooperative Library System), Charles W. Robinson (Baltimore County Public Library), Elliot Shelkrot (Pennsylvania State Library; Free Library of Philadelphia), Eleanor Jo Rodger (Fairfax County, Va., Public Library; Enoch Pratt Free Library; PLA), James H. Fish (Springfield, Mass., City Library), Kathleen Balcom (Downers Grove, Ill., Public Library).

Study Team

Using the framework outlined by the New Standards Task Force and responding to their guidance, the Study Team wrote the two manuals published by ALA Publishing Services and specified the design of the Public Library Data Service, now (June 1987) in preparation for implementation in early 1988.

Principal investigator, Charles R. McClure (University of Oklahoma; Syracuse University)
Nancy A. Van House (University of California–Berkeley)
Amy Owen (Utah State Library)
Douglas L. Zweizig (University of Wisconsin–Madison)
Mary Jo Lynch (Office for Research, American Library Association)

Test Sites

A number of libraries were selected by the Study Team as test sites to evaluate the usefulness and practicality of both manuals. As a result of the staff time and attention to the assignment, the Study Team received many valuable suggestions—suggestions which have made the manuals more valuable to those who will use them. Additional libraries, not listed here, are continuing to contribute to the success of the program by testing questionnaires of the Public Library Data Service. The test sites and coordinators are:

Alameda County (Calif.) Public Library—Ginnie Cooper; Newark Branch—Pat Zahn; Union City Branch—Linda Harris
Arlington Heights (Ill.) Memorial Library—Frank Dempsey
Clearwater (Fla.) Public Library—Carolyn Moore
DeKalb Library System (Ga.)—Donna Mancini
Denver (Colo.) Public Library—Rick J. Ashton
Iowa City (Iowa) Public Library—Lolly Eggers
Oakland (Calif.) Public Library—Lelia White
Oklahoma Department of Libraries—Sandy Ellison
Portland–Multnomah County (Ore.) Library—Sarah Long
Providence (R.I.) Public Library—Annalee Bundy
Salt Lake City (Utah) Public Library—Dennis Day
Spokane (Wash.) Public Library—Betty Bender
Springfield (Mass.) City Library—James Fish
Topeka (Kans.) Public Library—Bonnie Campbell
Washington County (Utah) Library—Russell Shirts
Wauwatosa (Wis.) Public Library—Margaret McGowan
Wilbraham (Mass.) Public Library—Paula Polk.

Photographs

The following libraries contributed photographs of staff members and library users for this publication:

Baltimore County Public Library
Los Angeles County Public Library
Phoenix Public Library
Skokie (Ill.) Public Library
Springfield (Mass.) City Library

Contributors

The Public Library Development Program is completely funded by state library agencies and individual public libraries across the nation. The nearly $200,000 contributed so far (April 1987) is, as far as we know, the most significant financial effort made to date in support of a cooperative project with no direct federal grants or foundation support. These libraries have reason to be proud of their support.

State Library Agencies

Alabama	Missouri
Alaska	Montana
Arizona	Nebraska
Arkansas	New Jersey
California	New York
Colorado	Oklahoma
Connecticut	Pennsylvania
Florida	Rhode Island
Hawaii	South Carolina
Indiana	South Dakota
Iowa	Tennessee
Kansas	Utah
Louisiana	Virginia
Maryland	Washington
Massachusetts	Wisconsin
Michigan	Wyoming
Mississippi	

Library Associations

Arkansas Library Association
Canadian Library Association
Connecticut Library Association
Illinois Library Association
Ontario Library Association
Pennsylvania Library Association, Southern Chapter
Rhode Island Library Association
Springfield (Mass.) Library and Museums Association
Texas Library Association
Wilton (Conn.) Library Association

Public Libraries

Abington (Pa.) Free Library
Alachua County (Fla.) Public Library
Alexandria (Va.) Public Library
Allen County (Ind.) Public Library
Amherst (N.Y.) Public Library
Ashtabula County (Ohio) District Library
Atlanta-Fulton (Ga.) Public Library
Baltimore County (Md.) Public Library
Bangor (Maine) Public Library
Bethlehem (Pa.) Public Library
Birmingham (Ala.) Public Library
Bloomfield Township (Mich.) Public Library
Bloomingdale (Ill.) Public Library
Boulder (Colo.) Public Library
Boynton Beach (Fla.) City Library
Brookline (Mass.) Public Library
Brooklyn (N.Y.) Public Library
Broward County (Fla.) Library
Bucks County (Pa.) Free Library
Buena Park Library District (Calif.)
Buffalo and Erie County (N.Y.) Public Library

Bur Oak Library System (Ill.)
Carnegie-Stout (Iowa) Public Library
Carroll County (Md.) Public Library
Cary Memorial Library (Mass.)
Cass County (Miss.) Public Library
Champaign (Ill.) Public Library
Cheltenham Township Library System (Pa.)
Cherokee County (S.C.) Public Library
Chester County (Pa.) Library
Chicago (Ill.) Public Library
Chickasaw Public Library System (Okla.)
Clark County (Nev.) Public Library
Clearwater (Fla.) Public Library
Cleveland Heights (Ohio) Public Library
Cobb County (Ga.) Public Library
Public Library of Columbus and Franklin County (Ohio)
Crystal Lake (Ill.) Public Library
Cumberland County (Pa.) Public Library
Dallas (Tex.) Public Library
Daniel Boone Regional Library (Mo.)
Dauphin County (Pa.) Library System
DeKalb Library System (Ga.)
Denver (Colo.) Public Library
Detroit (Mich.) Public Library
Dougherty County (Ga.) Public Library
Downers Grove (Ill.) Public Library
Durham County (N.C.) Library
East Baton Rouge Parish (La.) Library
East Orange (N.J.) Public Library
Englewood (Colo.) Public Library
Enoch Pratt Free Library (Md.)
Elyria (Ohio) Public Library
Escondido (Calif.) Public Library
Evansville–Vanderburgh County (Ind.) Public Library
Fairfield (Conn.) Public Library
Findley–Hancock County (Ohio) Public Library
Finkelstein Memorial Library (N.Y.)
Framingham (Mass.) Public Library
Fresno County (Calif.) Free Library
Gail Borden Public Library District (Ill.)
Geauga County (Ohio) Public Library
Genesee District Library (Mich.)
Grand Rapids (Mich.) Public Library
Granite City (Ill.) Public Library
Harford County (Md.) Library
Hartford (Conn.) Public Library
Harvey (Ill.) Public Library
Haverhill (Mass.) Public Library
Hennepin County (Minn.) Library System
Hildebrand Memorial Library (Wis.)
Holyoke (Mass.) Public Library
Houston (Tex.) Public Library

Huntington Beach (Calif.) Public Library
Huntsville (Ala.) Public Library
Indianapolis–Marion County (Ind.) Public Library
Iowa City (Iowa) Public Library
Jefferson County (Colo.) Public Library
Jefferson Parish (La.) Library
Joliet (Ill.) Public Library
Kansas City (Kans.) Public Library
Kansas City (Mo.) Public Library
Kilsap Regional Library (Wash.)
Lake County (Ind.) Public Library
Lake Lanier Regional Library (Ga.)
Las Vegas–Clark County Library District (Nev.)
Lexington (Ky.) Public Library
Lincoln (Neb.) City Libraries
Lisle Library District (Ill.)
Long Beach (Calif.) Public Library
Los Angeles County (Calif.) Public Library
Madison (Wis.) Public Library
Marin County (Calif.) Free Library
Metropolitan Library System (Okla.)
Miami-Dade (Fla.) Public Library
Mid-Hudson Library System (N.Y.)
Middle Georgia Regional Library
Milan (Mich.) Public Library
Milwaukee (Wis.) Public Library
Mobile (Ala.) Public Library
Mt. Prospect (Ill.) Public Library
Nevada County (Calif.) Library
New Hanover County (N.C.) Public Library
New Orleans (La.) Public Library
New York (N.Y.) Public Library
Newark (N.J.) Public Library
Norfolk (Va.) Public Library
Northbrook (Ill.) Public Library
Oak Lawn (Ill.) Public Library
Oakland (Calif.) Public Library
Ocean County (N.J.) Public Library
Oceanside (Calif.) Public Library
OCLC Inc.
Omaha (Neb.) Public Library
Onslow County (N.C.) Library
Oshkosh (Wis.) Public Library
Osterhout Free Library (Pa.)
Palm Springs (Calif.) Public Library
Palo Alto (Calif.) City Library
Pikes Peak Library District (Colo.)
Peoria (Ill.) Public Library
Free Library of Philadelphia (Pa.)
Phoenix (Ariz.) Public Library
Pioneer Multi-County System (Okla.)
Carnegie Library of Pittsburgh (Pa.)

Portsmouth (Va.) Public Library
Prince George's County (Md.) Memorial Library
Prince William County (Va.) Library
Providence (R.I.) Public Library
Queens Borough (N.Y.) Public Library
Redwood City (Calif.) Public Library
Richland County (S.C.) Public Library
Roanoke City (Va.) Public Library System
Rochester (Minn.) Public Library
Rochester Hills (Mich.) Public Library
Rosenberg Library (Tex.)
Roseville (Mich.) Public Library
Salt Lake City (Utah) Public Library
San Bernardino County (Calif.) Library
San Diego County (Calif.) Library
Santa Clara County (Calif.) Library
Santa Fe Regional Library (Fla.)
Scranton (Pa.) Public Library
Sioux Falls (S.D.) Public Library
Skokie (Ill.) Public Library
David R. Smith (consultant)
Southeastern Libraries Cooperative (Minn.)
Southern Maryland Regional Library
Spartanburg County (S.C.) Library
Spokane (Wash.) Public Library
Springfield (Mass.) City Library
St. Charles Public Library District (La.)
St. Cloud Great River Regional Library (Minn.)
Stoughton (Mass.) Public Library
Suffolk County (N.Y.) Cooperative Library System
Sunnyvale (Calif.) Public Library
Taunton (Mass.) Public Library
Tucson (Ariz.) Public Library
Tulsa City-County (Okla.) Library
Turner Subscriptions
Twin Falls (Idaho) Public Library
Ventura County Library Service Agency (Calif.)
Vigo County (Ind.) Public Library
Virginia Beach (Va.) Public Library
Volusia County (Fla.) Public Library; Deltonia, Holly Hill, Ormond Beach, and S. Cornelia Young Memorial branches
Watertown (Mass.) Free Public Library
Waukegan (Ill.) Public Library
Way Public Library (Ohio)
Weber County (Utah) Public Library
Webster Parish (La.) Library
West Bloomfield Township (Mich.) Public Library

West Hartford (Conn.) Public Library
Western Massachusetts Regional Library System
Westerville (Ohio) Public Library

Wicomico County (Md.) Free Library
Willows (Calif.) Public Library
Wissahickon Valley (Pa.) Public Library
Worthington (Ohio) Public Library

About This Book

This manual is about using measurement to evaluate public library services. It defines a set of measures relevant to common public library goals and gives detailed instructions for using them. It also discusses the uses of measurement in public library management, gives guidance on choosing measures, and makes suggestions for interpreting the data.

This second edition of *Output Measures for Public Libraries* developed from discussions with libraries that had used the first edition, an assessment of the data obtained using the first edition, and a trial of a draft of this revised manual in several libraries. The measures remain the same in this new edition. The changes:

- Some methods have been revised to make them easier or more appropriate.
- The discussion of each measure has been expanded to help readers understand what the data mean.
- Information on measurement, measurement methods, and interpretation and use of the results has been added.
- Measurement and evaluation is more closely intergrated with the process presented in *Planning and Role Setting for Public Libraries* (Charles R. McClure, Amy Owen, Douglas L. Zweizig, Mary Jo Lynch, and Nancy A. Van House. Chicago: American Library Association, 1987; hereafter referred to as *PRSPL*).

Libraries that already have data collected using the first edition of *Output Measures for Public Libraries* can continue to use the same measures. Their existing data will be comparable with data collected using this edition. However, they should switch to the procedures described in this edition. They will probably find that this edition answers some questions and eases their tasks somewhat. This edition does recommend generally larger sample sizes, however, in the interest of more accurate data. Slight changes in results from one year to the next as the library changes editions of the manual may occur as a result. These may be due, not to changes in library performance, but to the slightly more accurate results that these methods give.

Audience

This manual is intended primarily for small libraries (with at least one full-time professional staff member), medium-sized libraries, regional systems, and for state library agencies to use for public library development. Smaller libraries (less than one full-time professional staff member) may find that some of these measures require too much staff time, although they may find some useful ideas to adapt to their circumstances. Such libraries are especially encouraged to work with their state library agencies or regional systems to make the best use of this manual. Very large libraries may need more information than these measures will provide, although most branches of very large libraries are similar to small and medium-sized libraries and can use these measures effectively. The information in this manual may serve as a beginning from which the measurement effort can expand.

Not everyone involved in the data collection effort needs to read this entire manual. Each chapter states for whom it is most appropriate. Where measurement is being done in conjunction with the planning process, all members of the planning committee should at least skim this entire manual.

Purpose

The purpose of this manual is to define a basic set of output measures for public libraries that are widely applicable, relatively easy to use, at least partially under library control, comparable across libraries, and easily interpreted by the community. This manual presents detailed information on how to choose among these measures and how to collect, analyze, and interpret the data. For these measures to be useful, decision makers must understand what the measures mean about library services. Therefore the emphasis in this manual is on not just how to collect the data, but how to determine what the data mean and what to do about them.

Public libraries differ, and so do their measurement needs. A secondary purpose of this manual is to provide some understanding of measurement in general so that readers know when and how they can (or cannot) expand, extend, and adapt these measures. It also includes some suggestions and examples of additional measures and analyses that may better meet local needs.

Overview of the Manual

The organization of this manual follows the steps in the measurement process. Chapter 1 is concerned with evaluation in general and with selecting the measures to be used. Chapter 2 is about organizing the data collection effort. Chapter 3 presents basic information about collecting and analyzing data, and Chapter 4 is about interpreting and using the results. Chapter 5 goes through the measures one by one. For each measure it gives its definition, how it is calculated, instructions for collecting and analyzing the data, and further possibilities for going beyond the basic measure. The appendix contains copies of all the worksheets, suitable for photocopying.

This manual has been designed to be self-help. It requires no expertise in mathematics or statistics, and no equipment more complex than a calculator. It cannot be stressed too strongly that *the quality of the measurement data depends directly on carefully following instructions in this manual*. These instructions are quite detailed to make the process as easy as possible and to ensure good results.

Increasing Library Excellence

There is no magic formula for library excellence—many factors contribute to the quality of a public library. But regardless of the specific situation of a particular library, some basic prerequisites are needed. First, librarians must be able to describe accurately the existing library conditions and performance. Second, they must have a vision of what the services of the library should be. And finally, they must be able to design and carry out activities to reach this vision, and to evaluate their success in reaching it.

Taken together, *Planning and Role Setting for Public Libraries* and *Output Measures for Public Libraries,* second edition, provide tools for librarians wishing to increase the excellence of their libraries. Use of these two manuals on an ongoing basis will provide a framework within which the library's vision of excellence can be nurtured and realized.

NANCY A. VAN HOUSE   MARY JO LYNCH
CHARLES R. MCCLURE   DOUGLAS L. ZWEIZIG

January 1987

Introduction

The challenge of contemporary public librarianship is to achieve excellence despite rapidly changing needs and opportunities. In meeting this challenge, librarians are faced with difficult decisions about making effective use of resources. What is needed is a vision of what the library is to do and the skill to bring this vision about.

Planning and evaluation are important tools for achieving excellence in library services. Planning is the process of deciding where the library is going and how it will get there. It consists of studying the library and its community, choosing roles, defining a mission, setting goals and objectives, and designing activities to meet those ends. Planning is described in a companion to this volume, *Planning and Role Setting for Public Libraries* (Charles R. McClure, Amy Owen, Douglas L. Zweizig, Mary Jo Lynch, and Nancy A. Van House. Chicago: American Library Association, 1987; hereafter referred to as *PRSPL*).

Evaluation is the feedback loop of the planning process. It provides the information needed to keep the library headed in its chosen direction. Evaluation consists of comparing "what is" with "what should be." Planning determines "what should be." Information about "what is," the library's current performance, comes from a variety of sources: formal and informal, quantitative and qualitative. One source of this information is measurement.

Measurement is the collection, analysis, and organization of objective, quantitative data. Measurement is no-fault. It does not in itself indicate whether the library is "good" or "bad," it simply describes what is. What the data mean about the library's performance depends on the library's mission, goals, objectives, and circumstances.

This manual is about the use of output measures to evaluate public library services. Output measures reflect results or outcomes, the effectiveness and the extensiveness of the services delivered by the library. This manual describes in detail twelve relatively easy and generally useful output measures. But, perhaps more important, this manual is about interpreting and using measurement data to improve library services.

This chapter provides some general information about measurement and its uses in public libraries, plus some guidance on selecting measures to use from those described in Chapter 5. The primary audience for this chapter is the people deciding about measurement, especially those choosing which measures to use in their library. In most cases, this is library management. Where this manual is being used in conjunction with *PRSPL,* the library will have a planning committee which may also play a role in these decisions, and for whom this chapter is also intended.

Measurement in Public Libraries

Measurement serves several purposes in libraries:

- Assessing current levels of performance
- Diagnosing problem areas
- Comparing past, current, and desired levels of performance
- Monitoring progress toward the library's mission, goals, and objectives.

The most obvious benefit of measurement is the information it provides for planning and evaluation. Additional benefits include:

- Describing the library's performance to people

and organizations outside the library (local government, state library agency, the public, etc.)

- Demonstrating the library's commitment to planning, evaluation, and effectiveness
- Justifying (internally and externally) resource allocations
- Documenting service improvements
- Creating within the library an emphasis on activities as means toward ends (goals) rather than as ends in themselves.

Some examples of uses that libraries have made of the measures in the *Output Measures for Public Libraries,* first edition:

- One library pinpointed reference as a problem service area, which they then made a priority for improvement through staff development, reference collection development, and procedure analysis and revision.
- A library identified collection deficiencies (through analysis of the Materials Availability Survey responses) and each year chose subject areas for additional collection development.
- A central library demonstrated that use of materials within the library was very large relative to circulation and justified additional shelving staff during a time of citywide staff cuts, on the grounds that existing collection resources were not being effectively used because of shelving backlogs.
- A county library system demonstrated that users were not finding materials they needed and received a substantial one-time allocation for collection improvement.
- A library that had based branch staffing on circulation added in-library use and reference transactions to its basis.

Measurement and the Planning Process

Decisions about measurement are best made within the context of planning. Which measures to use depends on what information is needed for decision making, and on how well the measures reflect the library's mission, roles, goals, and objectives. This manual generally assumes that measurement is being done as part of a planning process such as that described in *PRSPL,* but this manual can be used by itself. Libraries can and do measure without planning, and plan without measuring. Some libraries plan first, and measure later; others measure first, and plan later.

Measurement enters into planning at several of the stages described in *PRSPL:*

Looking Around: This step consists of collecting and reviewing information about the library and its community. The measures in this manual are a major source of information describing the library's services.

Roles and Mission: Chapter 4 of *PRSPL* describes a set of Public Library Roles, or profiles of service emphasis, to help libraries choose the roles they play in their communities and define their mission. Each role description includes one or more "Output Measures to Explore" from this manual that may be useful in determining how well a library is fulfilling this role. Data on these measures may be useful in choosing roles as well as in determining progress toward the roles selected.

Goals and Objectives: Perhaps the most important use of output measures is in writing measurable objectives and monitoring library performance (see Chapter 5 of *PRSPL*). Measures are concrete indicators of the library's performance. The measures in this manual reflect common public library services. Not all libraries will use all these measures, and not all the measures they will use are here. But this core set (plus the suggestions under "Further Possibilities" in Chapter 5) will be generally useful, and can serve as models for locally developed measures.

Taking Action: In this step, the library determines what actions it will take. The measures identified in the objectives can be used to monitor the success of activities.

Reviewing Results: The measures can be used to assess how well the library is progressing, and whether its roles, mission, goals, objectives, or activities need to be reconsidered.

Some options for coordinating planning (formal or informal) and measurement include:

- Begin a planning process such as that described in the *PRSPL.* As part of Looking Around, select and collect data for the measures desired by the planning committee.
- Begin by collecting data for the measures that library management finds most relevant. Then start the planning process.
- Complete the planning process, using some of these measures in writing objectives. Then collect data on these measures to monitor progress.
- Choose the measures from this manual that your library finds the most relevant, collect and ana-

lyze the data, and use them in your usual decision making.

Overview of the Measures

Chapter 5 presents each measure in detail. In the following summary, the measures are categorized by the library's major services.

Library Use

These measures reflect the extent to which the library is used by its community.

- **Annual Library Visits per Capita** is the average number of library visits during the year per person in the area served. It reflects the library's walk-in use, adjusted for the population served.
- **Registration as a Percentage of Population** is the proportion of the people in the area served who are currently registered as library users. Although registration does not necessarily reflect use, the measure reflects the proportion of the people who are potential library users who have indicated an intention to use the library.

Materials Use

Libraries provide materials in many different formats for use inside and outside the library.

- **Circulation per Capita** is the annual circulation outside the library of materials of all types per person in the legal service area.
- **In-Library Materials Use per Capita** is the annual number of materials of all types used within the library per person in the area served.
- **Turnover Rate** measures the intensity of use of the collection. It is the average annual circulation per physical item held.

Materials Access

Library users need to be able to find what they are looking for. The first three of these are Materials Availability Measures, reflecting the extent to which users succeed in finding the materials that they need during their visit. The fourth Materials Access measure indicates how long people wait for materials not available at the time of their visit.

- **Title Fill Rate** is the proportion of specific titles sought that were found during the user's visit. It is not the proportion of users who were successful, because one user may have looked for more than one title; it is the proportion of the searches that were successful.

- **Subject and Author Fill Rate** is the proportion of searches for materials on a subject or by an author that were filled during the user's visit.
- **Browsers' Fill Rate** is the proportion of users who were browsing, rather than looking for something specific, who found something useful.
- **Document Delivery** measures the time that a user waits for materials not immediately available, including reserves and interlibrary loans. It is expressed as the percent of requests filled within 7, 14, and 30 days, and over 30 days.

Reference Services

Reference service consists of helping clients use information resources inside and outside the library and providing personalized answers to questions.

- **Reference Transactions per Capita** is the annual number of reference questions asked per person in the area served.
- **Reference Completion Rate** is the staff's estimate of the proportion of reference questions asked that were completed on the day they were asked.

Programming

Libraries provide programs to inform, educate, and entertain their clients and to promote library use.

• **Program Attendance per Capita** is the annual number of people attending programs per person in the area served.

Further Possibilities

In many cases, a library will want more information than is provided by these measures, for example, in a priority service area, or when a measure indicates a problem. In Chapter 5, "Further Possibilities" under each measure gives suggestions. These generally consist of one or more of the following:

• *Performing additional analyses of the data.* These are relatively easy. They generally require further analysis of the data that have already been collected (for example, analyzing the TITLES SOUGHT by subject). They may require larger sample sizes, however (see Chapter 3).

• *Constructing new measures from available data.* For example, Circulation per Hour Open is ANNUAL CIRCULATION divided by Hours Open, which is easily obtained.

• *Collecting more information and performing more extensive analyses.* For example, adding a question to the Materials Availability Survey

form asking whether users are adults, young adults, or children (or color-coding their survey forms), then calculating separate **Title** and **Subject and Author Fill Rates** for each group.

• *Taking advantage of additional local capabilities.* For example, libraries with automated circulation systems may be able to calculate **Turnover Rate** by subject area.

• *Collecting additional data.* For example, following up on unfilled requests on the Materials Availability Survey to find out why they were unfilled.

Special Client Groups

Most librarians will be particularly interested in further analyzing some data by client group. Many library services are targeted at particular groups, such as children and young adults. Evaluation of these services focuses on the special needs of these groups, on whether the library is reaching these populations, and on how well they are being served. In other cases, services may be targeted at the entire user population, but a better picture of service effectiveness will come from subdividing the client group and evaluating service to each group.

Virtually all libraries offer services targeted specifically at children and young adults. Other common client groups include people whose preferred language is other than English; people of specific ethnic/racial backgrounds; the homebound and institutionalized; people with disabilities; and the illiterate and newly literate.

Measuring service to some of these groups may require special considerations. Young children and people with limited skills in reading English, for example, may need help with the Materials Availability Survey, which is a written questionnaire.

The measures described in this manual are intended to reflect service to all users, not just adults, English-speaking people, and so forth. This should be kept in mind when planning data collection. Further analysis by client group is highly recommended in libraries where that information is appropriate.

Choosing Measures

Most libraries will use only a few of these measures to begin with, then perhaps add others as needed and feasible. The basic question to ask in choosing measures is: *Does the value of the information justify the effort?* You should collect only as much information as necessary, and collect the data that best support the decisions to be made.

The Value of the Information

The major use of measurement data is for planning and decision making, although the political uses of these data may be important, as well. Some questions to ask:

- Which measures best reflect our library's mission, goals, objectives? The most useful information for planning relates directly to these.
- What do we already know? Will the data tell us anything new? Or are our efforts better spent elsewhere? (But beware of thinking that you "know" more than you actually do.)
- What are our questions? Does a measure answer our specific questions? For example, **Circulation per Capita** measures the use of the collection outside the library. Measuring total use of the collection requires data on both **Circulation per Capita** and **In-Library Materials Use per Capita**.
- What difference would having data make in our decisions? If they would make no difference, do we really need the data?

- Once collected and analyzed, will the data actually be used?

Measurement data should not be collected simply for their own sake. Some data must be collected for state reporting requirements, grants, and the like, but data should not be collected simply to be put into reports that are never used.

Level of Effort

Some measures are easier than others. A library must consider how much effort it can devote to data collection overall, and to each measure individually.

The level of effort required by each measure depends on the source of the data; on whether sampling is used and, if so, the sample size; and on the length of time over which data are collected. Figure 1 summarizes this information for each measure. Chapter 5 contains more details and discussion.

Data Source: Common sources of data include:

- Existing data: Some data elements are generally available, either from library records (e.g., ANNUAL CIRCULATION) or from outside sources (e.g., POPULATION OF LEGAL SERVICE AREA). The easiest measures use existing data (e.g., **Circulation per Capita** is ANNUAL CIRCULATION divided by POPULATION OF LEGAL SERVICE AREA).
- Tally: Library staff count activities, items, or people. This requires a higher level of effort. Some tallies must be made at specific times; for example, staff count NUMBER OF REFERENCE TRANSACTIONS as they occur; other tallies can be made at the staff's convenience, for example, measuring HOLDINGS.
- User: The Materials Availability Measures require a survey of users. These are the highest level-of-effort measures. They require the most staff time to hand out, collect, and tally the questionnaires. They require the user's participation as well.

Sampling: Whenever possible, these measures are based on a sample of transactions or items. Sampling is often easier than counting everything. For example, sampling reference transactions for one week is easier than counting every transaction, every day, all year. It may also be more accurate. The sample size required depends on the uses to be made of the data, and the precision required (see Chapter 3).

Time Elapsed: Generally, the more time needed to collect and analyze the data, the

Measure	Data Element	Data Source Existing	Data Source Tally	Data Source Survey	Sample	Time Elapsed	Level of Effort[1]
Annual Library Visits per Capita	No. of Library Visits	[2]	X		Y	1 week	Higher
	Population	X			N		
Circulation per Capita	Annual Circulation	X			N		Low
	Population	X			N		
In-Library Materials Use per Capita	Annual Materials Use		X		Y	1 week	Higher
	Population	X			N		
Turnover Rate	Annual Circulation	X			N		Low
	Holdings	[3]	[3]		N/Y		
Title Fill Rate	No. of Titles Found			X	Y	2+ weeks[4]	Highest
	No. of Titles Sought			X	Y		
Subject/Author Fill Rate	No. Subj/Au Found			X	Y	2+ weeks[4]	Highest
	No. Subj/Au Sought			X	Y		
Browsers' Fill Rate	No. of Browsers Finding			X	Y	2+ weeks[4]	Highest
	No. of Browsers			X	Y		
Document Delivery	Document Delivery		X		Y	at least 60 days	Medium
Reference Transactions per Capita	Annual No. of Reference Transactions		X		Y	1 week	Medium
	Population	X			N		
Reference Completion Rate	No. of Reference Transactions Completed		X		Y	1 week	Medium
	No. of Reference Transactions		X		Y		
Registrations as Percentage of Population	Library Registrations	[3]	[3]		N		Low
	Population	X			N		
Program Attendance per Capita	Annual Program Attendance		X		N	1 year	Medium
	Population	X			N		

[1] Level of effort:
Low—Available data
Medium—Staff tally while going about their duties
Higher—Requires extra staff effort
Highest—Requires most staff effort

[2] Existing data, low level of effort if library has turnstile counter.
[3] Indicates more than one possible source.
[4] At least 1 week data collection; more time for analysis.

FIGURE 1 Overview of Measures and Data Collection Methods

greater is the level of effort. Time elapsed is also important in determining how rapidly the results will be available for decision making. If the data will be used in the planning process, for example, the planning schedule has to include time to collect and analyze the data. If the data are to be used to support the library's budget request, the library may face an immovable deadline. The only feasible measures will be those that can be done in the time available.

Level of Data Required: Multi-outlet libraries must decide whether results are needed for each outlet or branch, or only for the library as a whole. Results for each branch require more data, and therefore a higher level of effort, than results only at the library-wide level (see Chapter 3).

Valid, Reliable, and Comparable Results

To be useful, measurement results must be valid, reliable, and comparable. Valid measures do indeed reflect what they are intended to measure. For example, a library has an automated circulation system, but some special materials, such as phonograph records and videotapes, are not included in the automated system. The circulation figures provided by the automated system, therefore, are not a valid reflection of total library circulation: they are always incomplete. The circulation of materials not included in the automated system has to be added to that from the automated system to get a valid measure of total library circulation.

For measurement data to reliably reflect library performance, the same thing must be counted in the same way by everyone. Many of the measures in this manual rely on many people—staff and even the public—to collect the data. They must all be counting the same things in the same way. If, for example, one staff member counts directional transactions as reference questions and another does not, the number of reference transactions will vary depending on who is at the reference desk, rather than on the number of questions asked.

Measurement is usually used to make comparisons: to track a library's performance over time, or to compare it to others, such as other branches of the same library, nearby libraries, or "similar" libraries elsewhere. For comparisons to be made, the same things must be measured in the same way each time. If one library calculates **Turnover Rate** based on the total cat-

aloged collection, and another uses only the circulating collection, their results will not be comparable.

The instructions in Chapter 5 are very detailed to ensure reliability and comparability. *These instructions must be followed closely.* However, it is important to realize that:

- Everyone involved in data collection and analysis is capable of affecting the accuracy and the comparability of the data.
- This manual cannot anticipate and give instructions for every possible circumstance.
- Variations in measurement processes and in library operations will affect the comparability of the data.
- "Fine-tuning" the methods in this manual may reduce the comparability of your data with that from other libraries.
- Local decisions about data collection should be recorded and followed consistently by everyone involved in the data collection, and during every cycle of data collection.

The Process of Choosing Measures

Libraries using *PRSPL* may follow the processes outlined there to select measures. For example, Chapter 3 of *PRSPL*, Looking Around, describes a process for choosing the data to be collected. The measures in this manual should be considered at that time.

Figure 2 lists some questions that can be used with the information in Figure 1 to choose measures regardless of whether the library is using *PRSPL*. Added information about the measures and such items as sample size are in Chapters 3 and 5. Other criteria may be added as needed.

Before making final decisions, however, you should read the rest of this manual and at least skim Chapter 5 to understand the various measures and their data collection and analysis.

Special Situations

Small Libraries

Small libraries (one full-time professional or less) may be able to do only a few measures at any one time. You should pick a few easy measures to try first; you can add more later. Small libraries should also look to their state library agency and/or regional system for help. Small libraries have an advantage in being able to readily involve the entire staff in the data collection, analysis, and interpretation, thus im-

Use one worksheet for each measure being considered.

Measure: _____

Planned uses of this information (if in support of goals and/or objectives, list):

_____

_____

_____

Level of data needed:

System _____ Branch _____ Which branches? _____

_____

Additional data or analyses needed? Describe.

_____

_____

Date by which data needed: _____

Data collection method: _____

Sample size (if applicable): per branch and/or total:

_____

Estimated time required to collect and analyze data: _____

_____

Responsibilities:

Data Collection, overall: _____

Data Collection, actual collecting of data: _____

_____

Data Analysis: _____

Other: _____

_____

FIGURE 2 Measures Selection Worksheet

proving their understanding of the relationship between the measurement results and services.

These measures are not aimed at the library with less than one professional librarian. Smaller libraries are, of course, welcome to try any measures that seem useful and feasible. You, too, should consider getting help from your state library agency or a regional system.

Large Libraries

Large libraries may want to create additional measures of their own based on this manual. Large libraries often have more staff expertise for developing their own measures and methods and doing data analysis. You may also need more complex management information. The "Further Possibilities" under each measure in Chapter 5 may be particularly useful to large libraries.

Libraries with Multiple Outlets

Multi-branch libraries and multi-library systems are in some ways combinations of smaller libraries. Decisions are needed about which measures will be used at the library (or system) level and which at the outlet level (see Chapter 3 on calculating system and branch-level measurements). In addition, depending on the library, outlets or groups of outlets may be free to decide to use these measures on their own.

Once the decisions have been made about which measures to use, the library is ready to begin organizing its measurement effort. The next chapter is about managing measurement activities.

Sources for Additional Information

Lancaster, F. Wilfrid. *The Measurement and Evaluation of Library Services.* Arlington, Va.: Information Resources Press, 1977.

A good overview of measures and measurement methods for libraries.

McClure, Charles R., Douglas L. Zweizig, Nancy A. Van House, and Mary Jo Lynch. "Output Measures: Myths, Realities, and Prospects." *Public Libraries* 25 (Summer 1986): 49–52.

A discussion of the uses of output measures and measurement in public libraries.

Mason, Richard O., and E. Burton Swanson. *Measurement for Management Decision.* Reading, Mass.: Addison-Wesley, 1981.

A collection of readings on the uses of measurement in the management of organizations of all kinds.

Swisher, Robert, and Charles McClure. *Research for Decision Making: Methods for Librarians.* Chicago: American Library Association, 1984.

A comprehensive discussion of using measurement for library decision making.

Managing the Measurement Effort

Much of this manual, especially Chapter 5, is concerned with *what* the library does to collect and analyze measurement data. This chapter, however, is primarily concerned with *who* and *when:* with staffing and scheduling. It offers some guidance on designing and managing the data collection and analysis efficiently and effectively.

The primary audience for this chapter is the library managers most concerned with the logistics of the measurement effort.

Staffing

One person, the data coordinator, should be in charge of the overall data collection effort. Who it is that actually collects the data varies among the measures. Some libraries have made effective use of volunteers for some of the measures. It is important, however, that everyone engaged in the data collection be adequately trained.

The Data Coordinator

The data coordinator's responsibilities include:

• Planning and scheduling the data collection
• Designing or adapting data collection methods and forms
• Training
• Answering questions and handling problems
• Analyzing and reporting the data
• Ensuring uniformity in the data collection and analysis.

These responsibilities can be time-consuming, especially the first time that a library collects data for these measures.

Requirements for the person filling this position are:

• A good overview of the library's operations
• An understanding of how library management will use these data
• Organizational and communcations skills
• Rapport with staff in all parts and levels of the library
• An interest in the process.

A knowledge of statistics is not required, but an interest in numbers and measurement (and in computers, if one is available) will be especially helpful. If training in using this manual is available (e.g., from your state library agency), the data coordinator should attend.

If the library is also following the planning process described in *PRSPL,* the same person may oversee both measurement and the collection of other information for planning. In a library collecting substantial amounts of data, these may be two different people, but they should work together closely.

Data Collection

Some measures (see Figure 1) require that staff tally activities as they go about their daily work; for example, for **Reference Transactions per Capita** the staff count reference transactions as they are handled. For other measures, staff may be assigned to do the data collection, such as for **In-Library Materials Use per Capita**. Still other measures can be done with the help of volunteers, for example, the Materials Availability Measures. The discussion of each measure in Chapter 5 includes, when appropriate, who is to collect the data. Where the library can exercise some selectivity in the assignment of staff to data collection, it is important to consider the nature of the activity in choosing the staff. For example:

- Counting visitors for **Library Visits per Capita** requires no special skills but must be done conscientiously.
- Handing out Materials Availability Survey forms requires politeness, tact, and assertiveness.
- Measuring the shelflist to count HOLDINGS for **Turnover Rate** requires an understanding of the shelflist (for example, are phonorecords in a separate shelflist?).

Some libraries have made effective use of volunteers for some of the more time-consuming data collection, especially administering the Materials Availability Survey and counting visitors for **Library Visits per Capita**. Volunteers should be labelled in some way as being part of the library (for example a name tag or a badge with the library's name on it): users are often more cooperative when they know that the library is collecting the data.

It is especially important that volunteers be well-trained. They are often less familiar with the library and with the purpose of the data collection. For example, an unassertive volunteer (or staff member) may retrieve fewer Materials Availability Survey forms than one who is more forthright. This may bias the results.

Training

It cannot be stressed too strongly that *the quality of the data depends directly on people carefully following the procedures in this manual.* The detailed instructions in this manual are designed to make the process as easy as possible and to ensure uniform results. The people who collect the data—librarians, shelvers, circulation clerks, volunteers, and users—ultimately determine their quality.

The training needed in each library depends on the measures being used, the staff's existing skills and competencies, and the configuration of the library. Some possible training approaches are:

- Briefing sessions conducted by the data coordinator for the people doing the data collection, using handouts based on this manual
- Formal training sessions; for example, for the measures of Reference Services, sample questions are presented and discussed
- Trial runs and pretests, where the staff try out the data collection, then discuss their experi-

ences with the data coordinator before actual data collection begins.

Each person participating in the data collection should have access to a copy of this manual and know how to contact the data coordinator, who is the ultimate arbiter of any questions about data collection. Problems need to be resolved as they come up, and everyone affected should be informed.

A multi-outlet library collecting data in each outlet will need trained staff and a copy of this manual in each outlet.

Scheduling

Once the measures have been chosen (see Chapter 1), several scheduling questions remain before a library begins data collection, especially for the first time:

• Which measures to do when, including:

    Choosing sampling periods for the measures that require them
    Deciding which measures to do together and which separately

• Scheduling the data collection tasks: what to do and when
• And, finally, when does the library repeat each measure?

    Measurement as it is presented in this manual is a cyclical process. The data coordinator should develop an annual data collection schedule even

before the first data are collected. This can always be modified later. Approaching measurement as an ongoing process will help library management to decide what data to collect when.

Which Measures When

The measures that rely on existing data (see Figure 1) can be calculated at any time. Most libraries will want to tie those measures to their fiscal year, however. For example, for **Circulation per Capita**, the ANNUAL CIRCULATION used will be that for the most recently completed fiscal year.

SAMPLING PERIODS

For some measures, data are collected during a sample "typical" period: for example, **Reference Transactions per Capita** may be counted during a sample week. Figure 1 indicates which measures are based on samples.

    The times of the year during which data are collected should be representative of the rest of the year.* For **Library Visits per Capita**, for example, the easiest way to do this is to pick times that are neither very busy nor very quiet. Fall and spring are good times, but beware of the April tax form rush. Periods to *avoid* include summer, major holidays such as Christmas and New Year's, exam and vacation periods for local schools, and vacation periods for key library staff. For example, **Reference Completion Rate** may go down when a key reference staff member is away. Also avoid weeks with a holiday, and days when unusual events are taking place in the library: for example, when a large program will be bringing in many people only for the program.

DOING MEASURES TOGETHER AND SEPARATELY

The discussion of the measures in Chapter 5 indicates in some cases which measures are *best* done together and which *may* be done together. Some general concerns in deciding whether to schedule data collection for different measures at the same time are:

• Who is collecting the data? Staff limitations may preclude doing some measures at the same

---

*Technically, the results for such a sample period are an estimate of the results for that period of time only, not for the entire year: for example, measuring **Title Fill Rate** based on a sample of user searches in October is an estimate of the October **Title Fill Rate**. The rationale for picking a "typical" time period is that the library is assuming that the October **Title Fill Rate** is "typical" of the entire year.

time: for example, both the Materials Availability Survey and **In-Library Materials Use per Capita** require extra staff effort: the library may not be able to take on both at once.

- Where are the data being collected? Handing out and collecting Materials Availability Survey forms may create congestion at the door that will interfere with counting **Library Visits per Capita**.
- How are the data being collected? **Reference Transactions per Capita** and **Reference Completion Rate** may use the same form: they are most efficiently done simultaneously.
- Who is doing the data analysis, and how? If a lot of data collection over a short period of time will result in a bottleneck at data analysis, perhaps the data collection should be spread out more.

Some general guidelines for scheduling measures together include:

- The Materials Availability Measures (**Title Fill Rate**, **Subject and Author Fill Rate**, and **Browsers' Fill Rate**) should be done together. Not all libraries will do all three, but the data for whichever of the three are done are most easily collected all at once. These are the highest level-of-effort measures, and so the library may not be able to handle any additional data collection at the same time.
- **Reference Completion Rate** automatically provides the data for **Reference Transactions per Capita** (if Figure 40 is used) but not necessarily vice versa (if a library uses its own method of counting NUMBER OF REFERENCE TRANSACTIONS instead of Figure 40).
- **Library Visits per Capita** and the Materials Availability Measures may complement or interfere with one another, depending on how busy the library is (see the discussion under **Library Visits per Capita** in Chapter 5).
- **Document Delivery** takes longer than any other measure (except **Program Attendance per Capita**), but it can be done simultaneously with any and all other measures.

Scheduling the Data Collection Tasks

Once the decisions have been made about which measures will be done when, library management and/or the data coordinator can schedule data collection and analysis. Figure 3 presents a sample schedule showing a possible order to the tasks to be performed in implementing all the output measures. (The length of each phase will vary according to the library's circumstan-

Phase 1
Inform staff and board
Begin **Document Delivery** tally
Begin count of ANNUAL PROGRAM ATTENDANCE for **Program Attendance per Capita**
Record Data Elements already known (Figure 26)

Phase 2
Pretest Materials Availability Survey
Collect existing data as needed (such as measuring HOLDINGS for **Turnover Rate**

Phase 3
Conduct Materials Availability Survey

Phase 4
If necessary, gather data for **Library Visits per Capita**
Pretest data collection for **In-Library Materials Use per Capita**
Pretest data collection for **Reference Completion Rate** and **Reference Transactions per Capita**

Phase 5
Gather data for **In-Library Materials Use per Capita**
Gather data for **Reference Completion Rate** and **Reference Transactions per Capita**

FIGURE 3   Sample Tasking for Output Measurement

ces and resources.) Figure 4 is a scheduling form that can be used.

Some pointers on scheduling tasks are:

- The first time you use a measure, it is helpful to pretest the data collection in one branch or service unit to smooth out the procedures before the full-scale data collection begins.
- Be sure to allow enough time for data analysis: this is the task that libraries most often underestimate.

The Measurement Cycle

PRSPL presents planning as an ongoing activity. In the same way, measurement is most useful when repeated regularly, to show how service effectiveness is changing over time. An underlying assumption of this manual is that measurement will be repeated. How often data should be collected depends on the use to be made of the information, expectations about change, and the resources available for data collection. The more that the library and/or its community is changing, the more often measurements should be made. Problem areas may require more frequent monitoring than other areas.

Task	Person	Month											
		1	2	3	4	5	6	7	8	9	10	11	12
1.													
2.													
3.													
4.													
5.													
6.													
7.													
8.													
9.													
10.													
11.													
12.													
Notes and Explanations:													

FIGURE 4   Scheduling Chart

Regular data collection can be tied to planning and/or budget cycles. It will usually suffice to do each measure once every year or two (except when unusual changes are taking place). An annual report showing changes since last year is very useful for planning and budgeting. Annual objectives may then be set at the library and/or outlet level. This is discussed in *PRSPL,* Chapter 5.

Data may be collected less frequently than annually when it is intended to ensure that things have not changed, or to reflect activities that may take longer to affect services. For example, a library that is trying to improve its **Subject/Author Fill Rate** by changing acquisitions policies may wait two years for new materials to have a measurable impact before repeating the Materials Availability Survey.

Data for a given measure should be collected at close to the same time every year, and at the same time in each outlet, to ensure the comparability of the data across the years and among outlets. Not all measures need to be implemented at the same time, however. Some libraries do some in the spring, some in the fall.

Once the decisions are made about who will collect the data and when, the library is ready to move into the actual data collection and analysis. The next chapter provides some general guidelines on data collection, analysis, and reporting.

Data Collection, Analysis, and Reporting

The first two chapters have dealt with actions to take before collecting data. Chapter 4 is about interpreting and using the data. Chapter 5 presents detailed instructions for collecting and analyzing the data for each measure. The purpose of this chapter is to:

- Present instructions for data collection and analysis that apply to more than one measure in Chapter 5
- Explain the rationale behind some of the instructions in Chapter 5
- Present guidelines for analyzing the data
- Make suggestions for reporting the data.

The first part of this chapter is about collecting data for the measures in this manual. It discusses the sources of data for the measures and data elements, and gives general guidelines for collecting reliable, valid, and comparable data. It also gives instructions on selecting samples and determining sample sizes. The next part of this chapter is about analyzing the data, with special attention to libraries with multiple outlets. The last part makes suggestions for reporting the data so that they are useful and easy to understand.

The primary audience for this chapter is the data coordinator, for whom it is a necessary companion to Chapter 5. The planning committee (where one exists) and library management will find this chapter helpful in understanding the data and what they mean.

Data Collection

The data are the raw materials of the measures: the measurement results, therefore, are only as good as the data from which they are constructed. No special training in statistics or in research methods is required to collect data following the instructions in this manual. What *is* needed is common sense and an understanding of some reasons underlying the instructions in Chapter 5.

Guidelines for Data Collection

For data to be useful for decision making, they must be valid, reliable, and comparable over time. If they are to be used for comparisons across libraries or branches, they also need to be comparable across outlets. The following guidelines apply to all the measures in this manual:

- *Be consistent.* Count the same things in the same way regardless of when counted or by whom.
- *Decide in advance exactly what will be counted and how.* Record these decisions for future reference. Anticipating the decisions to be made guards against after-the-fact (and sometimes inconsistent) decisions.
- *Definitions, decisions, and methods should match those in this manual.* Consistency with this manual will ensure consistency within a library over time and with other libraries using this manual.
- *All staff who collect data need training and guidance.* The data are only as good as the people collecting them.
- *Minimize the impact of data collection on library services and users.* The priority is serving the user, not collecting data.
- *Minimize the obviousness of measurement activity* whenever possible. The more that people are aware of the measurement, the more

likely they are to be on their best (rather than their usual) behavior.

- *The more painless the count, the more accurate.* People won't bother counting if it is too difficult.
- *Allow time for learning.* It often takes people a while to learn what to count and how, and to remember when to count. Build a shake-down period into the schedule. Complicated procedures (such as the Materials Availability Survey) need trial runs to make sure that everything goes smoothly before starting actual data collection.

Data Sources

The data used by libraries comes from a number of different sources. The level of effort required to collect data varies by source. Figure 1 (in Chapter 1) lists the sources of the data for each measure and data element. The discussion below addresses some issues particular to each data source.

EXISTING DATA

Existing data are those that are already available, not collected specifically as part of the measurement process. They are the easiest to obtain. When available for past time periods, they can be used to track changes over time. They come from two general sources:

- From within the library: for example, ANNUAL CIRCULATION. Virtually every library already counts its circulation.
- From outside the library: for example, POPULATION OF LEGAL SERVICE AREA may come from the U.S. Census, local government, or state government.

Creative use of existing data from within and outside of the library will provide useful information with minimal effort. However, the library must thoroughly understand the data to be used; in particular:

- Do the data count what the library needs counted?
- Are the data accurate?
- Are the data consistent with the definitions in this manual?

Existing data often differ slightly from what is needed. For example, if fragile materials such as records are hand-charged, the circulation count from a circulation system may not count total circulation. All circulation transactions need to be included in ANNUAL CIRCULATION.

With internal data, the library generally knows what was counted and how, and can adjust for any differences from the definitions in this manual (for example, by adding in hand-charges and renewals). External data are more difficult because you may not know what you need to about the data. For example, different sources may give different population estimates for the same area. The library needs to know why these differ in order to pick the most accurate (e.g., U.S. Census figures are probably from the last decennial census, the Chamber of Commerce may add in nearby unincorporated areas, the state may adjust for recent population growth). (See also the discussion of POPULATION OF LEGAL SERVICE AREA in Chapter 5.)

TALLIES

For some data elements, items or activities are tallied by the staff, for example, ANNUAL IN-LIBRARY MATERIALS USE and NUMBER OF REFERENCE TRANSACTIONS. Many activities must be counted as they take place: for example, NUMBER OF REFERENCE TRANSACTIONS. This kind of data collection requires that many people do the counting (everyone who answers references questions), all of whom must know what to count and how. They must also understand the importance of recording every activity consistently. A missed transaction is lost forever.

Staff tallies at the time that an activity takes place may interfere with service delivery (or vice versa), so it is important that the counting method be as fast, easy, and convenient as possible.

When interpreting the data, one must consider that when the people providing the service do the counting, the results sometimes represent their best rather than their usual effort: we're all on our best behavior when we know our actions are being monitored. Furthermore, the very act of keeping a tally may improve staff performance by making them more aware of their actions.

SURVEYS

Libraries frequently survey the people who currently use the library. This is termed a user survey. The Materials Availability Survey described in Chapter 5 is a user survey that collects the information needed for the Materials Availability Measures: **Title Fill Rate**, **Subject and Author Fill Rate**, and **Browsers' Fill Rate**.

User surveys require that the library question a representative sample of people in the library. This is generally done by giving *all* users during

a defined period of time a written questionnaire.

Survey Administration: Surveys can be administered as either interviews or self-administered questionnaires. Interviews consist of questioning people directly and recording their answers. Self-administered surveys are written questionnaires. The Materials Availability Survey described in Chapter 5 is designed as a self-administered questionnaire; however, some libraries have done it as an interview. For users who find a self-administered questionnaire difficult (those with limited reading skills, non-English speakers, and sometimes children), an interview may be more appropriate.

The advantages of self-administered questionnaires include:

- They are generally much easier and faster for both the library and the user.
- They preserve the respondents' privacy, encouraging critical comments and frank answers.
- They eliminate possible interviewer effects on people's answers.

The advantages of interviews are:

- The questions can be more open-ended and the answers lengthier and more complex.
- If the interviewers are staff members, they may learn much about the library and its users.
- Interviews reduce the problems of respondents not following directions on a self-administered questionnaire.
- Interviews may have a higher rate of cooperation; it is harder to refuse someone directly than to not complete a questionnaire.

Interviewing is much more time-intensive, however. Furthermore, interview results may not be as valid as those from self-administered questionnaires because people may not be as straightforward in their answers. For example, users may be reluctant to criticize the library to a staff member.

Some guidelines for interviewing include:

- Interviewers must be trained so that each asks questions and records answers in the same way for the results to be comparable.

- Each interviewer should have a "script" beginning with something like "Good morning (afternoon, etc.), this library is conducting a survey and we would like to ask you a few questions"; listing all the questions to be asked, word for word; and concluding with "Thank you." Interviewers should not deviate from the script.
- Interviewers should record user responses exactly as given using a form much like a written questionnaire.

Before doing the Materials Availability Survey as an interview, consult some of the sources listed at the end of this chapter.

Survey Population: Survey respondents are a sample; for a user survey, only a few users are questioned, not everyone who uses the library. The following section on sampling discusses general issues. For a user survey, it is important that the people surveyed be representative of all the people who use the library. The instructions for the Materials Availability Survey in Chapter 5 are aimed at ensuring this. Periods of time are selected to represent as far as possible all the times of day and days of the week that the library is open. During those periods, *all* users are surveyed, not just those most willing to cooperate.

Inevitably, some users will refuse to cooperate, others will not return their questionnaires. Keep track of the response rate (the percent of users approached who accept and return legible questionnaires—see instructions for the Materials Availability Survey in Chapter 5). A low response rate (below about 60 percent) may mean that respondents are not representative. For example, perhaps only dissatisfied users are willing to participate. The data coordinator should also check to see that all kinds of users are being surveyed: for example, are children finding the survey too difficult? Are they getting adequate assistance in filling out their questionnaires?

Question Writing: Regardless of whether the survey consists of an interview or a self-administered questionnaire, the questions must be asked in a way that ensures valid and reliable results. The Materials Availability Survey form, Figure 33, has been designed, tested, and redesigned to ensure that it gives good results. It should be used without modification. The reader interested in questionnaire design should consult the sources listed at the end of this chapter.

Sampling

Sampling is the process of selecting a subset of a population (of people, objects, or events) from which to draw conclusions about the larger group. The key to sampling is that the group studied must be *representative* of the population to which the results are to be generalized. The guidelines presented here and in Chapter 5 are all aimed at ensuring representativeness.

Before selecting a sample, the population to be studied should be carefully defined. This is to ensure that the sample represents the larger population in which the library is interested. For example, if children and non-English-speaking adults are excluded from the Materials Availability Survey, then the results for the Materials Availability Measures do not apply to all library users, but only to English-speaking adult library users.

To avoid unintended biases introduced by the people drawing the sample, specific criteria are established, and every person, item, or transaction meeting those criteria is selected. This is why it is important to follow the instructions in this manual for the measures that use samples. For example, if the reference staff skip recording reference transactions when they are very busy, the **Reference Completion Rate** will only represent the level of service when the desk isn't very busy. But the **Reference Completion Rate** may be higher when the staff are less hurried, lower when they are busy.

SAMPLE SIZE

The immediate practical problem that arises when sampling is: How large a sample is needed? The larger the sample, the greater the level of effort. A library will want to use samples as large as necessary but no larger.

Samples result in estimates. The larger the sample, the more precise is the estimate, that is, the closer the sample result is to the true value (the population parameter, or the value that would have been derived from collecting data on the entire population instead of just a sample). The sample size needed depends on how accurate an estimate is needed.

Figure 1 indicates which measures use sample data. These fall into two categories:

- Those that estimate the number of activities or items:

  Library Visits per Capita
  In-Library Materials Use per Capita
  Reference Transactions per Capita

• Those estimating proportions or percentages:

> **Title Fill Rate**
> **Subject and Author Fill Rate**
> **Browsers' Fill Rate**
> **Reference Completion Rate**

(**Document Delivery** falls somewhere in between; the instructions in Chapter 5 explain how to determine its sample size.)

For the first group of measures, those estimating the number of activities or items, sample sizes have been developed and are described in Chapter 5. Generally, experience has shown that for most of these measures an adequate sample size is *one week's worth of transactions.* For **Library Visits per Capita**, for example, it is recommended that the library count visits for one week and multiply by 52 to estimate ANNUAL NUMBER OF LIBRARY VISITS.

For the second group of measures, those that reflect proportions, libraries can choose their sample sizes based on the precision of estimate that they need. For those that prefer not to choose their own sample size, *the recommended sample size is 400 transactions,* for example, 400 *each* of TITLES SOUGHT, SUBJECTS AND AUTHORS SOUGHT, BROWSERS, or NUMBER OF REFERENCE TRANSACTIONS—whatever the appropriate transactions are for the measure(s) to be used. For libraries that find 400 transactions excessive, smaller samples are acceptable, but *no smaller than 100 transactions of each kind.*

Using samples smaller than 400 results in less precise estimates. A less precise estimate may be sufficient, however. The choice of sample size should be based on the library's needs and the level of effort to be devoted to data collection. The next section explains what happens to the precision of the estimate with different sample sizes.

CONFIDENCE INTERVALS

Regardless of whether the library chooses its own sample size or uses the recommended size, to interpret the data you need to know how far off the estimate might be from the true value, that is, from the figure you would have obtained by collecting data for the entire population. The data coordinator will do the actual calculations (using Figure 6), but library management and the planning committee (where there is one) will find the following discussion helpful in understanding the results.

The possible difference between the estimate derived from a sample and the true value for the entire population is expressed using a confidence interval. The confidence interval consists of the value for the sample plus or minus the possible "play" or margin, that is, plus or minus the maximum possible distance that the estimate could be from the "true" value. The result is a range within which the "true" value falls.

Confidence intervals are expressed as the value derived from the sample, plus or minus the margin. For example, Figure 5 graphs **Title Fill Rates** for a group of branches. The shaded portion of each bar is the confidence interval. Branch A's **Title Fill Rate** is 75 percent plus or minus 5 percent, or between 70 and 80 percent. Branch A's **Title Fill Rate** is probably very close to 75 percent, but it could be as low as 70 percent or as high as 80 percent.

Confidence intervals are important because a simple **Fill Rate** may be misleading. For example, in Figure 5, Branch C's **Title Fill Rate** is 70 percent, so it appears that Branch C is not doing as well as Branch A. But actually the branch **Title Fill Rates** may be the same, because Branch A's **Title Fill Rate** confidence interval goes as low as 70 percent, and Branch C's goes as high as 75 percent. So they could actually be the same, somewhere in the range of 70 to 75 percent. The same would apply to a library that got a **Title Fill Rate** of 75 percent, plus or minus 5 percent, one year, and 70 percent, plus or minus 5 percent, the next. Service levels may not actually have changed from one year to the next.

The size of the margin depends on the size of the sample and the results obtained. *The smaller the sample, the greater is the possible margin in the estimate.* The next section tells you how to figure out what your margin is. The point is that the sample size only need be large enough to create a confidence interval that meets the library's needs: the less precision the library needs, the smaller the sample that will suffice.

The methods that follow are appropriate for **Title Fill Rate**, **Subject and Author Fill Rate**, **Browsers' Fill Rate**, and **Reference Completion Rate**. For simplicity, the term **Fill Rate** is used in the discussion below.

The first section below is for libraries that want the simplest approach. At a higher level of effort, the library can determine the precision of its estimate, that is, the width of its confidence interval, by adjusting its sample size. This is covered in the second section below, Calculating Sample Sizes.

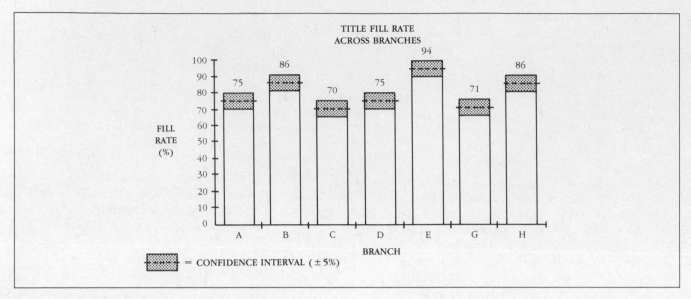

FIGURE 5 Comparing Confidence Intervals

USING THE SUGGESTED SAMPLE SIZE

For the **Fill Rates**, this manual suggests *a sample size of 400 transactions for each of the measures.* If 400 transactions are more than the library can feasibly handle, the sample can be smaller, but *no smaller than 100 transactions.* That is, for **Title Fill Rate** we recommend between 100 and 400 TITLES SOUGHT; for **Subject and Author Fill Rate**, between 100 and 400 SUBJECTS AND AUTHORS SOUGHT; between 100 and 400 BROWSERS for **Browsers' Fill Rate**; and between 100 and 400 REFERENCE TRANSACTIONS for **Reference Completion Rate**. These should be collected over a period of no more than two weeks. (For more on this, see the instructions for the Materials Availability Survey in Chapter 5.)

Remember that these sample sizes refer to usable transactions. One Materials Availability Survey form, for example, may contain more than one TITLES SOUGHT and SUBJECTS AND AUTHORS SOUGHT, and may or may not represent a BROWSER.

After collecting the data and calculating the **Fill Rate(s)** following the instructions in Chapter 5 of this manual, use Figure 6 to figure the confidence interval for each measure.*

---

*Figure 6 is at an 80% level of confidence. This is lower than is customary for research, but probably adequate for management decision making. At this level of confidence, we can say that, in the long run, 80% of the confidence intervals obtained using this method will include the true (population) parameter.

To use Figure 6:

1. Find the sample size closest to yours across the top. Your sample size is the total number of transactions of this kind in your sample (e.g., TITLES SOUGHT, SUBJECTS AND AUTHORS SOUGHT, BROWSERS, or REFERENCE TRANSACTIONS). Your goal may have been 400 (or 100), but you may have ended up with more or fewer.
2. Down the left side of the table, find the **Fill Rate** closest to yours.
3. The figure at the intersection of these two is your margin.
4. Your **Fill Rate** interval is between the figure that you calculated from your survey results PLUS your margin, and that same figure MINUS your margin.

> *Example:* A library's users report 200 TITLES SOUGHT. Sixty percent were filled. Using Figure 6, the margin for 200 at 60 percent is 4 percent. The true **Title Fill Rate** for this library is 60 percent plus or minus 4 percent, or between 56 and 64 percent. The confidence interval for this library's **Title Fill Rate** is 56 to 64 percent.

CALCULATING SAMPLE SIZES

Calculating your own sample size is slightly more complex than using the suggested sample size. It is most appropriate for libraries that have used a measure before and want their estimate to fall within a specified range.

1. Estimate what the **Fill Rate** is likely to be

(from previous years' data, from neighboring libraries, or from an informed guess).

2. Decide what size margin you need and find it in Figure 6 in the row with the expected **Fill Rate**.

   a. The size margin you need depends on how precise an estimate you need: is plus or minus 5 percentage points acceptable, or do you need plus or minus 3 percentage points?

3. The sample size at the top of that column is the target. (*Remember that these are usable transactions*; see the instructions for the Materials Availability Survey in Chapter 5 to translate this to MAS questionnaires.)

4. After the data have been collected and analyzed, it is likely that the final **Fill Rate** and/ or sample size is not quite what you expected. Use the method under Using the Suggested Sample Size, above, to calculate the margin from the actual data.

   Example: The same library decides the next year to determine its own sample size. It expects its fill rate to go down to about 55 percent because its new materials budget was cut. It wants to bring its margin down to plus or minus 3 percent. Using Figure 6, it needs 400 TITLES SOUGHT (between 50 and 60 percent fill rate, 3 percent margin).

A more precise estimate requires a progressively larger sample size. *There is a direct trade-off between level of effort and precision.*

MULTIPLE OUTLET SAMPLE SIZES

In a library with branches, a decision must be made about the results needed:

1. One figure for each measure for the entire library taken together, or
2. A figure for each branch individually as well as the library as a whole.

Once this decision has been made, the data coordinator uses the discussion that follows to determine sample sizes.

For the measures for which the library counts transactions during one week, each outlet simply collects data for a week; how those data are combined to a system-level result is explained below under Data Analysis. For the **Fill Rates**, this decision affects the total sample size and how the sample is distributed among the branches.

Branch-level Results: Using the recommended sample sizes, each outlet should have

Fill Rate %	Sample Size					
	100	200	300	400	500	600
10%	4%	3%	2%	2%	2%	2%
20	5	4	3	3	2	2
30	6	4	3	3	3	2
40	6	4	4	3	3	3
50	6	5	4	3	3	3
60	6	4	4	3	3	3
70	6	4	3	3	3	2
80	5	4	3	3	2	2
90	4	3	2	2	2	2

NOTE: Based on a 2-tailed test, 80% confidence level

Example: A library with a sample of 300 and a **Title Fill Rate** of 60% has a margin of 4%. The confidence interval for its **Title Fill Rate** is 56% to 64%.

FIGURE 6 Margin of the Fill Rate Estimate

a minimum of 100 transactions (400 is better). If you calculate your own sample size, use the method described above under Calculating Sample Sizes, repeating for each branch individually. To calculate the overall library-level measure from the branch samples, see, under Data Analysis below, Outlet and Library-level Data.

Overall Library-level Only: The sample size required for the library as a whole is either the recommended sample size (preferably 400 but at least 100), or is calculated using the methods described under Calculating Sample Sizes. *Then the sample is distributed among the branches according to their relative shares of total system activity* (the first four columns of Figure 7 can help):

1. Use the previous year's circulation data to determine the percentage of system activity contributed by each branch.

   Example: Total ANNUAL CIRCULATION for the system was 100,000. The Main Library's circulation was 75,000, or 75 percent. Branch A's circulation was 25,000, or 25 percent.

2. Determine the sample size needed using either the recommended sample or the method above for calculating your own.
3. Multiply the sample size by the percent of circulation for each branch to determine how many transactions should come from each

This form can be copied and used to calculate **Subject and Author Fill Rate**, **Browsers' Fill Rate**, and **Reference Completion Rate**, as well.

Branch	Annual Circulation	% of System Circulation	Target Sample Size[1]	TITLES SOUGHT	TITLES FOUND
System Total				(1)	(2)

Library Title Fill Rate: (2)/(1) = _____%

[1] Multiply total library-level sample size by each branch's percentage of total library circulation.

FIGURE 7   Calculating Library-level Title Fill Rate (*not* Branch Level)

branch. This is the target sample size for each branch.

> *Example:* The library needs a sample of 400 to determine its **Title Fill Rate**. 300 TITLES SOUGHT (75 percent) should come from the Main Library, 100 from Branch A.

Simply distributing the sample equally among the branches, without correcting for activity levels, would give smaller branches a disproportionate influence on overall results. Smaller branches contribute less to the total volume of system service and so should count proportionately less. Analyzing these data is discussed below.

Data Analysis

Data analysis is the process of summarizing the results of the data collection in usable form. The only math required to analyze the data for the measures in this manual is addition, subtraction, multiplication, and division. Figure 27, Output Measures Summary Sheet (in the Appendix), shows how to calculate each measure, and Chapter 5 contains the necessary directions.

The only equipment required for computing results is a simple calculator. Computers may sometimes be useful but are not essential. Spreadsheet software or statistical packages may be helpful, especially when combining the results for multiple branches or service desks, calculating trends over time, and producing graphics.

Libraries with Multiple Outlets

In a library with branches, data analysis can be done centrally or each unit can do its own, with outlet-level results combined and reported centrally. As with data collection, consistency is essential: *everyone should follow the same procedures in doing the data analysis.*

When a library is composed of many branches, the library-level measures are constructed from the results from the different outlets. Overall library service is composed of services delivered at the different branches. The underlying rule for constructing library-level measures, therefore, is that *each branch should contribute to the library-level measures in proportion to its contribution to library-wide services.* The following directions explain how to do this.

LIBRARY-LEVEL DATA ONLY

The sample size determination for overall library-level results described above under Multiple Outlet Sample Sizes distributes the sample size among the branches in proportion to their share of total library circulation. The overall library results can then be calculated by simply adding together the raw data for the various branches. For example, Figure 7 shows how to calculate **Title Fill Rate**; Figure 7 can simply be copied and also used to calculate **Subject and Author Fill Rate**, **Browsers' Fill Rate**, and **Reference Completion Rate**:

1. Add together the TITLES FOUND from all the branches.
2. Add together the TITLES SOUGHT in all the branches.
3. Divide 1 above by 2 above. The result is **Title Fill Rate** for the library as a whole.

If the actual sample size (number of usable TITLES SOUGHT, SUBJECTS AND AUTHORS SOUGHT, and/or BROWSERS) for each branch is much different from the target sample size (Figure 7), adjust for this by weighting the branch results using the instructions under Outlet and Library-level Data presented below. However, if your sample is less than 100 transactions from each branch, *calculate only the library-level result, not one for each branch.*

Determine the confidence interval for each

Fill Rate from Figure 6, using as the sample size the total number of searches for all branches combined.

OUTLET AND LIBRARY-LEVEL DATA

Branch-level results require an adequate sample size for each branch. In consolidating the branch measures into an overall library measure, however, the branches must be represented in proportion to their contribution to overall library services. *Under no circumstances can you simply average the results without weighting for branch activity levels.* If you did, the smallest branches would count as heavily as the largest, even though the smaller branches account for many fewer transactions.

Figure 8 is an example of calculating branch and system level results. Figure 8 is for **Title Fill Rate**, but can be adapted to other measures by replacing the data elements at the heads of the columns. Using Figure 8:

1. Determine each branch's required sample size using either the suggested sample size (400; minimum, if necessary, of 100) or the instructions under Calculating Sample Sizes.
2. Use the method described above under Library-level Data Only to determine each branch's proportion of system circulation.
3. Calculate each branch's results from its own data (e.g., each branch's **Title Fill Rate**).
4. Multiply each branch's **Fill Rate** by its proportion of system circulation. The result is Weighted Title Fill Rate.
5. Add together all the Weighted Title Fill Rates for each branch for a Library **Title Fill Rate**.
6. When reporting each branch's **Title Fill Rate**, use column 4 of Figure 8, *not* Weighted Title Fill Rate (column 5).

Example: The Main Library does 50 percent of the system's circulation. The Main Library's **Title Fill Rate** is 70 percent. Weighting this by 50 percent: $.7 \times .5 = .35$. North Branch does 38 percent of system circulation. Its **Title Fill Rate** is 60 percent. Weighting this by 38 percent: $.6 \times .38 = .23$. South Branch's Weighted Title Fill Rate, calculated in the same way as North's, is .06. The library's **Title Fill Rate** is $.35 + .23 + .06 = .64$, or 64 percent.

If not all branches participated in the data collection, use the total circulation *only* for the branches that did participate to calculate each branch's percentage of annual circulation. Then use these new percentages to calculate weighted results.

This form can be copied and used to calculate **Subject and Author Fill Rate**, **Browsers' Fill Rate**, and **Reference Completion Rate**, as well.

Branch	Annual Circulation	% of System Circulation (1)	TITLES FOUND (2)	TITLES SOUGHT (3)	Title FR (2)/(3) (4)	Weighted Title FR (1) × (4) (5)

Library-level **Title Fill Rate**: total of column (5) = _____%
(must be less than 100%)

FIGURE 8 Calculating Branch *and* Library-level Title Fill Rates

Reporting the Results

The results of the data collection and analysis data need to be communicated in a way that the audience can readily understand. The audience may include library management, staff, the planning committee, and the library board (where these exist). It may also be local government officials and members of the community.

PRSPL offers some suggestions for presenting data collected as part of planning. See, in particular, Chapter 3, Looking Around.

The report may be short and simple or longer and more complex. Some options in varying the level of effort in reporting the data are presented in Figure 9. The simplest and most universally useful report is a summary sheet with the data for all the measures (Figure 26). This summary is more useful, however, when it shows more than one year's data, and shows changes over time (Figure 10). Where the library has adopted an objective incorporating a measure, the desired outcome is entered in the column headed "Objective." At a more extensive level of effort, this report can incorporate text discussing the results and plans for the future.

Outlet Data

A multi-outlet library with outlet-level measures may need a summary for each branch or outlet (using Figure 10, for example). The report may include some input measures, such as collection, staff FTE (full-time equivalents), and square footage, for comparing branch resources.

Another approach is to report all the data, or only those for a few related measures, for all the outlets on one summary sheet. Figure 37 in the Appendix is an example of such a summary for the measures derived from the Materials Availability Survey. This approach facilitates branch comparisons.

It may also be useful to compare outlet results for specific measures:

- Add a column to the report with the branch ranking on that measure. For example, the branch with the highest value for a given measure is ranked 1; the second highest 2; etc.
- Group the branches whose values on a given measure fall within a certain range. For example, group 1 might be all the branches with a **Title Fill Rate** over 70 percent; group 2, 60 to 70 percent; etc.
- Sort the branches into groups of equal size according to their values for a given measure. Example: create four groups, each with 25 percent of the branches in it. The first group is the 25 percent with the highest **Circulation per Capita**; group 2 the next highest 25 percent, and so on.

Graphics

Graphics can be a powerful means of presenting data. They are much more readily understood than numbers. Many libraries now have personal computers with good graphics software and printers.

Figure 11 is a bar graph. This is a useful way of comparing across branches and/or over time. Figure 12 is a line graph, showing trends over time.

Once the data have been collected, analyzed, and reported, library management and the planning committee (where applicable) are ready to sit down and review the results for what they mean for this library. This is the subject of the next chapter.

Sources for Additional Information

Babbie, Earl R. *Survey Research Methods.* Belmont, Calif.: Wadsworth, 1973.
     A practical, readable how-to on surveys.
Busha, Charles H., and Stephen P. Harter. *Research*

Basic Level of Effort

- Summary sheet with results from each branch (where applicable) for current and past year (Figure 10)
- Selected resource measures, such as:

    Expenditures

    Holdings

    Staff FTE

Moderate Level of Effort: <u>add</u> to the above

- Background on data collection

    Sample sizes

    Short description of procedure used for data collection

    The time periods during which data were collected

    Any difference between data collection methods used and those in this manual

- Brief discussion of the results

Extensive Level of Effort: <u>add</u> to the above

- Detailed description of data collection, including samples of data collection instruments
- Extensive discussion and interpretation of the findings (see Chapter 4)
- Graphics to illustrate the data

FIGURE 9 Suggested Format for Reporting the Measurement Results

Library _____

Date _____

Measure	Objective	Current FY	Last FY
Browsers' Fill Rate[1]			
Circulation per Capita			
In-Library Materials Use per Capita			
Library Visits per Capita			

Document Delivery:
  within 7 days
  within 14 days
  8 to 14 days
  15 to 30 days
  more than 30 days			

Program Attendance per Capita			
Reference Completion Rate[1]			
Reference Transactions per Capita			
Registration as a Percentage of the Population			
Subject and Author Fill Rate[1]			
Title Fill Rate[1]			
Turnover Rate			

[1] Enter upper and lower limits of confidence interval as well as the actual figure derived from the data; for example, 60% ± 5%.

FIGURE 10 Library/Branch Measurement Report

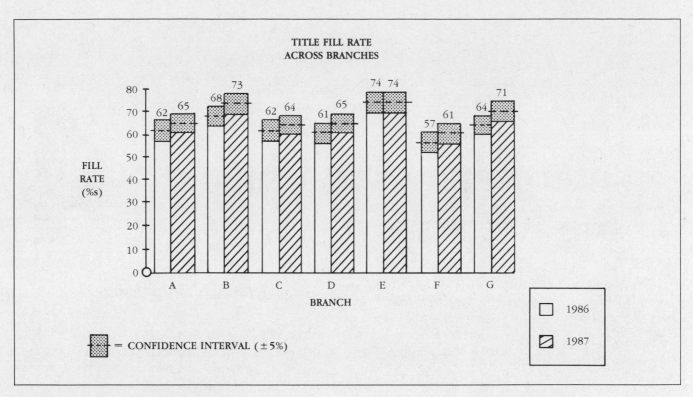

FIGURE 11 Sample Bar Graph

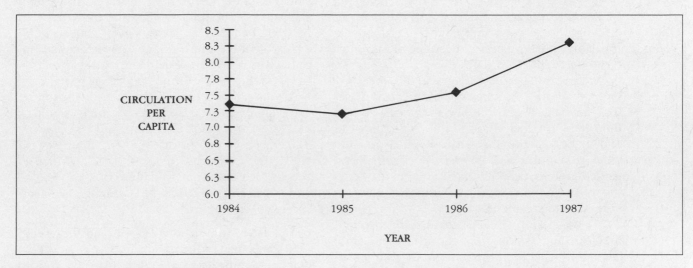

FIGURE 12 Sample Line Graph

Methods in Librarianship: Techniques and Interpretation. New York: Academic Press, 1980.

Reviews major data collection and analysis methods for libraries.

Hernon, Peter, and Charles R. McClure. *Microcomputers for Library Decision Making.* New York: Ablex, 1986.

An introduction to microcomputers for library management data.

Martyn, John, and F. Wilfrid Lancaster. *Investigative*

Methods in Library and Information Science: An Introduction. Arlington, Va.: Information Resources Press, 1981.

Discusses numerous data collection methods that have been used in libraries.

Swisher, Robert, and Charles McClure. *Research for Decision Making: Methods for Librarians.* Chicago: American Library Association, 1984.

Using data collection and analysis for library decision making.

Interpreting and Using the Results

At this point, the library has selected some measures, collected and analyzed the data, and reported the results. Now what? What do the data mean? What can you do about them?

The data themselves describe the library's current state without indicating whether it is "good" or "bad." Furthermore, these measures do not describe every aspect of the library and its services. They are, instead, a few vital signs, to be combined with other quantitative and qualitative information from a variety of sources on which to base evaluation and decision making. This chapter gives some suggestions for interpreting a library's data.

Once a library has learned about measurement and collected some baseline data describing library services, measurement can add an important dimension to the library's operations and management. But to do so, measurement must be ongoing and the data must actually be used. Another task at this point, therefore, is incorporating measurement into the library's ongoing management.

The discussion of each measure in Chapter 5 includes suggestions for what the data might mean and what the library might do to improve its results. This chapter offers some suggestions for interpreting the results more generally, in the context of the library's own circumstances; for making comparisons over time and across libraries; and for using the data in planning, formal or informal. The last part of this chapter is about incorporating on-going measurement into library management.

This chapter is aimed primarily at library management and the planning committee (where there is one), the library's decision makers. It will also be useful to the data coordinator and to library management in planning continued measurement.

Relationships among the Measures

The library is a system of interrelated components. Each measure is a snapshot of this system from one perspective. Depending on the angle from which the picture is taken, some features are emphasized, while others are deemphasized or even hidden completely. A three-dimensional picture requires that these individual snapshots all be put together and the spaces in between be filled in. Each measure reflects only a part of library performance. Overreliance on only one or a few measures could lead to the library doing very well in some areas but poorly in others not reflected in the measures used.

It cannot be stressed too strongly that the measures are interdependent and should be looked at as a set. Although not all libraries will use all the measures, the data that are available should be looked at together. Chapter 5 discusses possible relationships among the measures. For example:

- High **Title, Subject and Author, and Browsers' Fill Rates** may indicate satisfied users; but they may also indicate a collection that is not being used, so that when a user does look for something, everything is on the shelf. The Materials Availability measures should be coupled with the Materials Use measures, such as **Circulation per Capita**, for a more complete picture of library use.
- Increasing **Reference Transactions per Capita** without increasing staffing may decrease **Reference Completion Rate** because the staff will have less time to spend on each question.

Librarians have not had enough experience with these measures to understand completely the interactions among them. These possible relationships must be considered in the context of the individual library. And some important relationships may not be mentioned in this manual. The planning committee and/or library management should consider carefully possible interrelationships among these measures in *their* library.

The Context

Output measures occur in a complex organizational and political context. They reflect the performance of both the library and the user. The interpretation of the measurement results is not automatic. This is a chance for the planning committee, library management, and staff to engage in some creative thinking about the library.

Interpreting the measurement results requires a consideration of a number of contextual factors, including:

- The library's roles, mission, goals, and objectives
- The library's resources
- The community.

Roles, Mission, Goals, and Objectives

Generally, the first questions that people ask when they see their library's measurement results are, "Is that good? Are we doing well?" We cannot answer these questions without specifying, "Good with regard to what?" The answer to which is, "Good with regard to what the library wants to accomplish," that is, the library's role, mission, goals, and objectives. *PRSPL* emphasizes that each library chooses these for itself.

PRSPL emphasizes the need for a library to set priorities. In measurement terms this means that a library cannot expect to maximize its performance on all measures at the same time. In choosing roles and writing a mission statement, and especially in writing objectives, a library decides which measures (from among these and other measures) are most important, and what levels of performance it wants to achieve.

A library that has not engaged in a formal planning process and/or does not have written goals and objectives will still interpret the measurement results according to what it set out to accomplish. These results can form the basis for discussions about what are the library's goals and objectives, which measures should be monitored regularly, and in what areas performance should improve.

The Library's Resources

The library's performance is constrained by its resources. When interpreting the data, consider the library's staff, materials, building, budget and other resources, and resource sharing. Some of these factors may be targeted for change as a result of planning and evaluation; some may be fixed constraints within which the library must live.

Short-term conditions may temporarily affect measurement results. For example, the illness of a key staff member may reduce the level of services provided by a branch; the conversion to an automated circulation system is inevitably temporarily disruptive; and so on. In considering the long-term implications of the output measures, librarians should ask themselves whether such temporary factors are making the data unrepresentative of library performance overall.

The Community

Library performance depends on the match between library resources and services and user needs. Social, economic, and demographic characteristics of the community affect the demands placed on the library. Because much library use is self-service, service outcomes are also critically dependent on people's ability to use the library. Measurement results need to be considered in the context of the community that each library serves. Again, the information collected during Looking Around (or similar information in libraries not using *PRSPL*) is needed to fully understand the meaning of the measurement data.

Comparisons

The discussions of the individual measures in Chapter 5 talk about "high" and "low" values without defining what is high and what is low for a given measure. This is deliberate because "high" and "low" depend on circumstances and a particular library's objectives.

Libraries that have used *Output Measures for Public Libraries,* first edition, have found that one way to make sense out of their data is to make comparisons. The most useful comparison is with a library's own performance at an earlier time: are we doing better or worse than last year? Other possible comparisons are across branches within a library, and among "similar" libraries.

In making comparisons, however, it is important to understand that differences in measurement methods, in the the community served,

• The precision of the data affects comparisons. If a library's **Title Fill Rate** one year is 55 percent with a 5 percent margin (see Chapter 3), and the next year it is 60 percent, again with a 5 percent margin, one *cannot* conclude that the **Title Fill Rate** has improved. The two years' confidence intervals (the sample fill rate plus or minus the margin) overlap, and so the two years' values may be the same (see Figure 5). Generally, *small changes in the values of the measures that use sampling may not indicate real changes.* Conversely, the measures that use sampling cannot detect small changes in library performance. As discussed in Chapter 3, trade-offs must be made between the level of effort and precision of these measures. For this reason, it is especially important to look at the pattern of results across measures and over time rather than at only one or two scores.

• Conditions within and outside the library may change over time and affect the results. Library staff's actions are only one factor affecting the measurement results. For example, in a rapidly growing suburb the number of school children served may increase dramatically in a short period, taxing the library's children's services and affecting **Fill Rates**.

Across Outlets

Another common comparison is across branches or member libraries of the same system. Different communities have different needs and make different demands on their libraries. People with different educational backgrounds may differ in the kinds of information that they need from their library and the kind of assistance that they need in using the library. Branches may have different resources and different goals and objectives. For example, small branches may not expect a high **Reference per Capita** because they may not be equipped to handle much reference service. All these contextual factors need to be considered in comparing branches within the same system.

Across Libraries

A useful comparison is with "similar" libraries. This often means libraries serving similar communities. However, libraries also have different missions, goals, and objectives. These will affect their service priorities, which will generally be reflected in their measurement results. "Similar" libraries should be defined, therefore, not only by demographics, such as population, age

and in the library's resources and actions may show up as differences in the measurement results.

Over Time

The easiest and most useful comparison is with a library's own performance over time. A library collecting data consistently over several years can track trends and note the effects of various library activities. The measures in this edition have been kept compatible with those in the first edition of this manual so that libraries can compare the results achieved using the two editions.

In making comparisons over time, however, remember:

• The data must have been collected consistently. Changes in definitions or procedures make the results noncomparable.

• Staff learning may affect the comparisons. Inevitably, after the first measurement cycle, staff will better understand data collection and analysis and the uses to which the data will be put. And methodological problems may be found and resolved.

distribution, and income, but also by library roles (see *PRSPL,* Chapter 4), and resources, including holdings, staff, and operating expenditures.

Acting on the Results

Measurement results are used to make decisions about the library's roles, mission, goals, objectives, and actions, and to evaluate the choices already made. These uses are encompassed by the planning process described in *PRSPL.* Libraries that are not engaged in formal planning, or are not following the *PRSPL*'s process, can still use these results in much the same way.

Using the Results in Planning

Chapter 1 of this manual discusses the relationship between measurement and the planning process, and the uses of these data at various phases of planning; for example:

- *Looking Around:* You now have additional information about current library performance. Are you pleased with the results? Surprised? Disappointed? Have you discovered some areas in need of improvement?
- *Developing Roles and Mission:* If your library is not performing well on a measure important to one of its chosen roles, perhaps you should rethink, not only what you are doing to fulfill that role, but also whether your library can and should emphasize that role.
- *Writing Goals and Objectives:* A major use of these measures is in writing your objectives. Which measures should your library be using in its objectives? What levels of performance will you set for your library?
- *Taking Action:* How well is the library doing on its objectives? Are the actions chosen having the expected results? The discussion of "Analysis and Use of the Data" under each measure in Chapter 5 suggests possible actions to improve library performance.
- *Reviewing Results:* How well is the library progressing toward its roles, mission, goals, and objectives, as reflected in the measures? Do the original roles, goals, and objectives need fine-tuning or revision?

A library not currently engaged in formal planning and wondering how to use these data to improve library services may want to consider planning as the next step. *PRSPL* describes several levels of planning effort. You need not engage in any more complex an undertaking than you can handle.

Other Uses of the Results

Some other actions to undertake with the data, especially in libraries not currently engaged in formal planning, include:

- *Bring the staff together to discuss the implications of the data.* Are you satisfied with the library's performance on the various measures? Do the results indicate any problem areas? Why does Branch A have a higher value on a measure than Branch B? Should Branch B be more like Branch A? Think about the results.
- *Write or revise goals and objectives using these measures.* What levels of performance do you expect of your library? This can be done by the director, by a management team, by a committee, whomever. See *PRSPL,* Chapter 5, for guidelines on writing objectives.
- *Consider possible actions to improve performance in areas where you are dissatisfied with the results.* Chapter 5 gives some examples for each measure.
- *Investigate problem areas turned up by the data.* For example, if you are dissatisfied with your **Reference Completion Rate**, appoint a task force to investigate causes and recommend possible solutions.
- *Communicate the results* widely within and outside the library. Remember that measurement has a number of benefits, including:

    Giving staff feedback on the library's performance

    Fostering a results orientation among library staff

Demonstrating to the community the library's commitment to results.

- *Review the measurement results with local officials.* The results will communicate the library staff's interest in service quality, and may form a basis for useful discussions about the library's role in its community.
- *Review the measurement results with state library agency and/or regional library system staff.* They may have useful insights about the results' meaning and possible actions.

These measures are *not* meant to reflect individual staff members' performance, and do not replace personnel evaluation.

Figure 13 answers some questions that often come up at this stage.

What if we find no difference in our measurement results from one year to the next, despite our efforts to improve our performance in those areas?

- The measures, especially those collected using samples, may not be sensitive enough to reflect small changes in performance of your library.
- Rethink the validity of your measures: are you looking for change in a measure that does not actually reflect what you have accomplished in your library? For example, your **Title Fill Rate** may be the same but your **Circulation per Capita** may have increased, reflecting a higher overall level of service.

We were surprised by the data. We just don't believe that our performance is that poor (or that good).

- Perhaps your impressions were wrong. People tend to remember extreme performance (good and bad); perhaps your library's performance is not what you thought.
- Check your data collection and analysis. There may have been mistakes or misunderstandings.
- If you used a sample or a survey, the problem may have been with when you collected the data, or your response rate, or the size or representativeness of your sample. Was something unusual going on? (One library's **Title Fill Rate** plummeted when the shelver responsible for new books was sick.)
- Remember that there may be trade-offs across the different measures. Perhaps your performance is better in one area and therefore not as good in another. Look at all the measures together.

We didn't find any differences across branches.

- Perhaps there are none. Staff and/or users may adjust their behavior to suit the circumstances. For example, users may not look for items that a branch is unlikely to have.
- Perhaps the measures are not sensitive enough to pick up small differences across branches.
- Were your data collection and analysis methods the same across branches?

We found surprising differences across branches.

- Were your data collection and analysis methods the same across branches?
- Perhaps the branches are more different than you thought.
- Remember that community and user characteristics, as well as library resources, can affect the results. Results may differ depending on, for example, the educational backgrounds of users.

FIGURE 13 Answers to Common Questions

Following Up

The worst thing to do with measurement data is to put them in a drawer and forget them. The library staff now have experience with data collection and analysis, and information on the library's performance. This is the time to plan the next data collection cycle, and to incorporate regular measurement into the library's ongoing management.

Planning for the Next Data Collection

Output measures are most useful when the library has more than one year's data, to look for trends and to correct for temporary aberrations. Some possible actions at this point include:

- Review the data and decide whether to add or eliminate some measures on the next cycle. Consider also the "Further Possibilities" in Chapter 5 for next time.
- Make notes on methods and procedures that you adapted or developed for your own library, or changes to be made next time.
- Establish (if you haven't already) a schedule for data collection: which measures, how often, at what times of year, at branch or overall library levels.
- Note any problems, discoveries, or ideas to help make the next measurement cycle go more smoothly, perhaps by annotating a copy of this manual.

Incorporating Measurement into Library Decision Making

Now that the library has baseline data, the same measures can be repeated periodically to track changes over time. The best way to ensure that measurement will be ongoing and that its results will be used to the greatest advantage is to incorporate measurement into the library's usual procedures and operations. The more that measurement is treated as "special" and "different," the less likely staff are to continue data collection, or to actually use the results.

Some examples of what other libraries have done are:

- *Give an individual or a committee ongoing responsibility for measurement.* This group may establish a measurement schedule, consider additional or alternative measures, develop im-

proved data collection methods for your library, etc.
- *Incorporate measures into your planning, budgeting, and reporting.* Use them for internal accountability and external reporting. Include them in your library (and, where applicable, branch) annual reports. Use them as a basis for budget allocations.
- *Have regular meetings of library managers* to discuss status of and progress on various output measures scores.
- *Write goals and objectives for next year incorporating these measures.* This can be at the regional system, library, branch, or department level. (See Chapter 5 of *PRSPL*.)
- *Require that proposals for new programs or activities include an evaluation component* using these or similar measures.

As library staff work with the measures, they will find additional uses for them. They may also devise additional measures that reflect what the library most needs to know.

The *process* of measurement has benefits beyond those of the data alone. Thinking and talking about the effects of their actions is beneficial for staff and management alike. A results orientation is necessary for innovation; not "We do this because this is what we do" but rather "We do this in order to achieve these ends. Are there better ways of reaching the same ends?"

Library Management and Measurement

Output measures are valuable tools for library management. They reflect the quality of library services and provide feedback on library activities. They are also powerful devices for communicating with the library staff and board, local government, and the community about what the library is trying to accomplish and how well it is doing. They describe what the library *is* doing, and can be a basis for discussing what it *should be* doing.

Measurement doesn't provide easy answers. One of its chief values is the additional questions that it raises: Why did we get those results? Are we satisfied with them? What can we do about them? These questions make people think and talk about the library. Measurement provides both the impetus and a factual basis for the discussion.

Librarians still need to learn more about the relationships among output measures, and the effects on output measures of library actions, resources, and community characteristics and circumstances. This manual cannot tell a library what it should be doing: all that it can do is to provide some methods for collecting data and some suggestions for using the data in decision making.

Perhaps the greatest benefit of measurement is not the data themselves but rather this way of thinking, an orientation toward results. It encourages library staff and decision makers to evaluate their actions in terms of goals and results. The inevitable result is a questioning of past practice: Have we been doing what is most effective in terms of our mission, roles, goals, and objectives? Are there better ways to accomplish the same ends? In this way, measurement can be the beginning (or part of) a more comprehensive approach to planning and evaluation.

The goal of planning and measurement is library excellence. These measures provide library decision makers with information to help them in their efforts to improve library services, to provide their communities with the best possible library services.

The Measures

This part of the manual presents each of the measures individually, arranged by library service. For each measure, it includes:

- Its definition.
- How it is calculated.

    Measures are calculated from more basic building blocks called data elements. Throughout this manual, measures are in bold type, and data elements are CAPITALIZED. For example, **Circulation per Capita** is composed of the data elements ANNUAL CIRCULATION and POPULATION OF LEGAL SERVICE AREA. Figures 26 (Data Elements Summary Sheet) and 27 (Output Measures Summary Sheet) show the relationships among data elements and measures and provide space to record your results.

- Analysis and Use of the Data: suggestions about what the results may mean, and possible approaches to improving a library's results. Whether a library wishes to increase or decrease its scores on a measure depends on the library's objectives. This discussion gives some suggestions to consider *if* the library wishes to change its results. These suggestions are only a few possibilities to spur thinking.
- Collecting the Data: detailed instructions and worksheets. Worked examples have been included for many measures. Blank worksheets are in Appendix A.
- Pointers and Special Considerations, where appropriate.
- Further Possibilities: suggestions for additional analyses of the data, data collection, and measures.

Those making the decisions (see Chapter 1) may want to read selected sections of this chapter before making final choices about which measures to use. This will give them an understanding of what each measure means, how the information might be used, and the effort required to collect the data. The most practical approach is for them to review the discussion for each measure that they have tentatively identified as being of interest. They may skim "Collecting the Data" under each measure in this chapter or skip it entirely until they are fairly certain that they want to use a specific measure. "Collecting the Data" has been placed near the end of each discussion to make it easy to skip.

For the data coordinator, this chapter is central to designing and implementing the data collection and analysis. He or she will want to use this as a reference. For the staff collecting the data, this chapter contains instructions and answers to questions, plus it will help them understand what they are doing and why. They should have access to the sections describing the measures for which they are collecting the data.

Population of Legal Service Area

POPULATION OF LEGAL SERVICE AREA is a data element used in many of the measures (Data Elements Summary Sheet, Figure 26, item p) to calculate per capita figures. It is the number of people in the geographical area for which a public library has been established to offer servies and from which (or on behalf of which) the library derives income, plus any area served under contract for which this library is the primary service provider. The Legal Service Area

may be a city, town, or county, or parts of one or more of these.

POPULATION OF LEGAL SERVICE AREA does *not* include residents of other jurisdictions with which your library has an agreement for reciprocal services. Nor does it include people who are served by another library but who secondarily receive service from your library under contract. Generally, a person is only counted once, in the population of one library, but not always; for example, people who are taxed at the local level to support more than one library are counted by each of the libraries that they support.

The population figure for a given Library Service Area may differ depending on the source of your data. The preferred sources for these data, in order, are:

1. Your state library agency
2. The state-level agency responsible for planning
3. Your local planning department
4. The *County and City Data Book* (which reports U.S. Census data)
5. U.S. Census figures from other sources (such as census reports).

Remember that U.S. Census data are updated only every ten years. Sources like the local Chamber of Commerce may not be very accurate: their estimates are often overly optimistic.

The purpose of the per capita adjustment is to express the results in terms of what is possible or needed: a library serving a small community is going to have a smaller circulation than one serving a larger community, but how do they compare relative to the population served? In comparing libraries or service out-

lets, other kinds of standardization may also be considered:

- Per hour the library is open (adjusts for differences in the availability of services)
- Per square foot (adjusts for the size of the building)
- Per volume (adjusts for the size of the collection)
- Per staff hour (adjusts for the staff resources available).

These can be used in addition to the per capita adjustment.

LIBRARIES WITH MULTIPLE OUTLETS

A special concern for libraries with branches is defining the POPULATION OF LEGAL SERVICE AREA for each outlet for outlet-level per capita measures. People inevitably cross whatever service lines the library may establish. Some possible approaches include:

1. Gather the branch librarians to discuss the areas served by each branch. Have them come to a consensus on where to draw the service area lines. Keep in mind traffic patterns—the branch that is easiest to get to is not always the closest. If you do this by census tract, you can use U.S. Census population data.
2. See if your local government has defined planning areas that roughly coincide with your branch distribution.
3. Have each branch sample about 200 registration records from the branch file (see Sampling, under Data Collection, in Chapter 3) and plot people's home addresses on a large map. Use these maps to draw branch service area boundaries.
4. Do the same as in 3 above, but use circulation records. This will show where the more frequent users live.

All these approaches only provide rough population estimates. Branch service areas are easier to define in some communities than in others; the library management know best how accurate their own population estimates are.

Central library per capita measures are especially difficult to compute. If the central library is treated like just another branch, it will have very large outputs per capita. If its population is considered to be that of the entire system, it will have low outputs per capita. The recommended solution is to use the population of the total library service area, knowing that this will result in low figures compared to the branches.

Library Use Measures

People use their libraries for a variety of purposes. Many of the measures that follow reflect the use of specific services. The Library Use Measures indicate the extent to which people use the library for all purposes.

• **Library Visits per Capita** measures the number of visits to the library each year in relation to the number of people in the library's service area.

• **Registrations as a Percentage of the Population** indicates the proportion of the people eligible to use the library who are registered.

Library Visits per Capita

Definition: Number of library visits during the year per person in the community served.

Calculation: ANNUAL NUMBER OF LIBRARY VISITS divided by POPULATION OF LEGAL SERVICE AREA.

Data Collection: Turnstile counter, or count people entering the building during one week.

All members of the public entering the library, for whatever purpose, are counted.

Example: A library serves a population of 25,482. It counts 140,151 LIBRARY VISITS during the year. The **Library Visits per Capita** is 5.5 (140,151 divided by 25,482).

Analysis and Use of Data

Of course, some people visit the library more than average, and some don't visit it at all. Some come into the library for reasons other than to use the library's collections and services. And some use the library without visiting it, for example, by telephone. This measure relates the number of visits to the library to the number of people who might use it.

One useful approach: compare this figure to the number of people attending sporting events in your community, using the parks, going to the movies, etc.

If you want to increase **Library Visits per Capita**, you might:

• Modify hours, perhaps more weekend and evening hours
• Increase the hours open
• Publicize the library more, stressing location, hours, and services available
• Increase the available parking
• Consider modifying your materials selection to better meet community interests.

Collecting the Data

A turnstile or other device that automatically counts people entering measures ANNUAL NUMBER OF LIBRARY VISITS.

For the library without a turnstile, two methods of data collection are possible. The library can simply count visits during a one-week sample period, and estimate ANNUAL NUMBER OF LIBRARY VISITS. In some cases, a turnstile can be rented for the week. Otherwise, you will need to place a person near the entrance to count people coming through the door. The other method is to count visits while doing the Materials Availability Survey (discussed later in this chapter).

ONE WEEK SAMPLE OF VISITS

1. Choose a sampling period following the instructions under Scheduling in Chapter 2. If possible, choose a week with no programs. Otherwise, choose a week with typical programs.
2. Have someone monitor each entrance and tally people as they enter. Figure 28, Library Visits Tally Sheet, counts visits by time of day. (Figure 14 is a worked example of Figure 28.) Many libraries prefer to break this count down further, by hour. However, all that is needed is a daily total. A counter that the person holds and "clicks" every time someone comes through the door can also be used.

a. This person generally cannot be doing anything else at the same time.

b. This person needs to be someplace where he or she won't be asked questions by patrons. This generally means that the person should not be at a service desk, and should not be too close to the door.

3. Multiply the weekly total number of visits by 52 to obtain the number of visits per year.

4. People who attend programs should be included in this measure. If your sample period excludes times when programs are held, add them in by doing one of the following:

   a. If the library counts ANNUAL PROGRAM ATTENDANCE, simply add that number to annual visits.

   b. If not, count the people attending in-library programs for the entire month during which the library visits are being counted, multiply by 12, and add to your annual visits figure.

5. Treat meeting room use in the same way as program attendance.

6. Add together annual visits, program attendance, and meeting room use. The result is ANNUAL NUMBER OF LIBRARY VISITS. Enter on Data Elements Summary Sheet, Figure 26, item c.

7. Divide by the POPULATION OF LEGAL SERVICE AREA (Data Elements Summary Sheet, Figure 26, item p) to obtain number of **Library Visits per Capita.**

VISITS AS PART OF THE MATERIALS
AVAILABILITY SURVEY

During the Materials Availability Survey (described in detail later in this chapter), all users entering the library during sample periods of time are given questionnaires. If the library can give a questionnaire to each user, or reliably count the number of people who do not get questionnaires (refusals, people who enter while the surveyor is busy with another visitor, etc.), then you know how many people visited the library during the sample period. From this you can calculate average number of users per hour, and multiply by hours open per year to estimate ANNUAL NUMBER OF LIBRARY VISITS.

However:

- Even small libraries may have very busy times (e.g., after school) when users arrive in groups and the surveyor cannot give everyone a ques-

tionnaire or even count the number of people entering the library.

- In large, busy libraries, the sample period required to hand out enough questionnaires may not be sufficiently long to safely extrapolate to the annual total. You should be counting visits for *a minimum* of three entire mornings, three afternoons, three evenings, and one entire Saturday and one entire Sunday (if applicable). See "Approximating This Measure," below.

Before a library uses this method of counting visits, it should at least do the Materials Availability Survey Pretest (described under Materials Availability Survey, below) to see if this approach is feasible. It would be even better to do an entire Materials Availability Survey at least once first.

Pointers/Special Considerations

- If a staff member does the counting, it is not recommended that you try to "correct" for people reentering the building, people only using the restrooms, and so forth. Since many libraries have turnstiles, and within a library some branches may have turnstiles and some may not, for ANNUAL NUMBER OF LIBRARY VISITS to be comparable across libraries or branches, a person should count the same people that a turnstile would, that is, everyone coming through the entrance.

- If you are using a one-week sample, it is not recommended that you adjust for the number of days the library is closed during the year, for example, by multiplying by something less than 52. Where data have been collected and compared, it appears that holidays may reduce visits slightly, but they also simply shift many visits to other days of the week.

Further Possibilities

- Analyze visits by time of day (morning vs. afternoon; or by hour). This is useful for scheduling. If you are using the Library Visits Tally Sheet, Figure 28, you can subdivide it by hour. If using a turnstile, record the turnstile counts periodically during a sampling period; for example, the difference between the counter at noon and at 5 p.m. is the number of visits during that time.

- Determine the percentage of walk-in users coming from outside the local service area by asking users during the sample period where they live. Do it as they leave, so that nonresi-

Date ___12/1/86___

Entrance ___Main___

Use one tally sheet each day. Enter number of hours during which data were collected.

A: Morning visits. Morning is from __9__ a.m. to noon, or __3__ hours.

	Total
HHT HHT HHT HHT HHT HHT HHT HHT HHT HHT HHT II	57

B: Afternoon visits. Afternoon is from noon to __5__ p.m., or __5__ hours.

	Total
HHT HHT HHT HHT HHT HHT HHT HHT HHT HHT HHT HHT HHT HHT HHT HHT HHT HHT III	93

C: Evening visits. Evening is from __5__ to __9__ (closing time), or __4__ hours.

	Total
HHT HHT HHT HHT HHT HHT HHT HHT HHT HHT HHT HHT HHT II	67

FIGURE 14 Worked Example of Figure 28: Library Visits Tally Sheet

dents don't feel threatened. The boxes on the Library Visits Tally Sheet, Figure 28, can be subdivided into resident and nonresident, or by jurisdiction.

• Analyze the number of visits by population groups, such as adults, young adults, and children. This requires observing and noting on the Library Visits Tally Sheet whether each user is an adult, a young adult, or a child. The observor will have to decide to which group each visitor belongs.

• Analyze the number of visits per public service

staff hour (e.g., two staff members working for one hour equals two staff hours).

• Create a new measure, Library Use per Capita, that adds telephone reference transactions, people served by outreach services (counting each visit to a homebound person, for example, as one use), etc., to ANNUAL VISITS, to include people who use the library without coming in.

• Create a new measure, Library Contacts per Capita, that adds in other community contacts for a more comprehensive measure of the library's impact on its community. Add in people attending meetings where library staff speak, for example, and students visited at school by library staff.

- **Library Visits per Capita** is often closely related to **Circulation per Capita**. Calculate both measures once, and determine the ratio ANNUAL NUMBER OF LIBRARY VISITS divided by ANNUAL CIRCULATION. This ratio can then be used to estimate ANNUAL NUMBER OF VISITS from ANNUAL CIRCULATION, which most libraries count. Every few years, both measurements should be done again and the ratio checked. (How often this needs checking depends on how stable use patterns are.)
- Count people's use of various library facilities: how many people use which facilities, and how

does that relate to what's available? For example, on average, what percent of the library's study space is in use? See Ernest DeProspo and others, *Performance Measures of Public Libraries* (Chicago: American Library Association, 1973).

Approximating This Measure

If you can't count for an entire week, the sample period may be shortened to three mornings, three afternoons, three evenings, one entire Saturday, and one entire Sunday (if the library is open then). Use Figure 29. If possible, *avoid periods with programs and/or meeting room use;* add those in separately, as instructed on Figure 29. (Figure 15 is a worked example of Figure 29.)

1. Total of all weekday morning visits made during the sample periods. (See Library Visits Tally Sheet, Section A)	(1) *183*
2. Number of weekday morning hours in the sample periods. (e.g., 3 hours Monday morning + 3 hours Wednesday morning = 6)	(2) *9*
3. (1) divided by (2) = average number of weekday morning library visits per hour.	(3) *20*
4. Number of weekday morning hours the library is open each week	(4) *15*
5. (4) × (3) = the estimated number of weekday morning visits per week	(5) *300*
6. Repeat steps 1–5 for (a) afternoon, (b) evening, (c) Saturday, and (d) Sunday visits and hours, and record the estimated number of (a) weekday afternoon, (b) weekday evening, (c) Saturday, and (d) Sunday visits per week	(6a) *680* (6b) *500* (6c) *850* (6d) *—*
7. (5) + (6a) + (6b) + (6c) + (6d) = the estimated number of visits each week.	(7) *2330*
8. Line (7) × 52 = average number of visits per year	(8) *121,160*
9. If not counted at the door, record the number of persons attending in-library programs for the entire month during which the door count is taking place and multiply by 12; OR enter annual meeting room use (if known).	(9) *500*
10. If not counted at the door, record the total number of persons using the library meeting room for the entire month during which the door count is taking place, and multiply by 12; OR enter annual meeting room use (if known).	(10) *600*
11. Add (8) + (9) + (10) to obtain the estimated ANNUAL NUMBER OF LIBRARY VISITS. Record on Data Element Summary Sheet, item (d).	(11) *122,260*
12. Divide (11) by POPULATION OF LEGAL SERVICE AREA (Data Element Summary Sheet, Figure 26) for **Library Visits per Capita**	(12) *5.4*

NOTE: This method to be used only if one-week sample is not possible. See text, "Approximating This Measure."

FIGURE 15 Worked Example of Figure 29: Estimate of Annual Number of Library Visits

This method is most feasible in libraries with very stable patterns of library use over time, which is usually large, busy libraries. The fewer the ANNUAL NUMBER OF LIBRARY VISITS, the greater is the effect of a random fluctuation in library use on such a sample, and the more it is recommended that the sampling period be one entire week.

One possible approach is: the first time through, use the entire one-week sample, collecting data by time of day. Then look at these results to see how different your annual estimate would have been if you had sampled for the shorter period of time. If the results would not have been very different, next time use the shorter period.

Registrations as a Percentage of the Population

Definition: Proportion of the people in the community served who have registered as library users.

Calculation: LIBRARY REGISTRATIONS divided by the POPULATION OF LEGAL SERVICE AREA.

Data Collection: Count number of registrations in library registration file.

Registration as a Percentage of the Population is a measure of the extent to which the library is reaching its potential user population, based on what proportion of them are registered.

Example: A library serves a population of 25,482. It has 15,300 LIBRARY REGISTRATIONS. **Registrations as a Percentage of the Population** is 60 percent.

Analysis and Use of the Data

LIBRARY REGISTRATIONS is difficult to measure reliably unless the library has an up-to-date automated file. Registration records need to be weeded regularly to provide an accurate count. Differences in registration periods and policies, such as cards for children and families and for nonresidents, create differences across libraries. *Therefore this measure is recommended for internal use only.*

Not all users are registered, and not everyone who is registered uses the library, but this measure does give an indication of the proportion of the community who use the library.

Possible approaches to increasing **Registrations as a Percentage of the Population** are:

• Publicize the library and its services better
• Engage in outreach to population groups that don't use the library as much as they might
• Consider whether the library's collection and

services could better match the community's needs.

Possible approaches to correcting **Registrations as a Percentage of the Population** include:

• Weed the registration file. Eliminate registrations that have expired.

Collecting the Data

LIBRARY REGISTRATIONS can be estimated in several ways.

1. If patrons must reregister annually, use this figure.
2. If patrons register for a two-year period, the number of people who register in a year is multiplied by two (e.g., $2 \times 2,420 = 4,840$).
3. If patrons register for a three-year period or longer (including "lifetime registrations"), the number of people who register in one year is multiplied by three (e.g., $1,623 \times 3 = 4,869$).
4. If a library continuously updates its count of registered borrowers by adding and deleting names, it may use its current registration figure. This may be obtained by counting registrations, or by estimating them. If a library keeps a manual registration file, and the file is too large to count, its size can be estimated using the same method used to measure the

shelflist. See Measuring the Shelflist under the discussion of **Turnover Rate** later in this chapter.

Pointers/Special Considerations

• Changes in registration policies, in the frequency with which the registration file is weeded, and the like will affect the results not only across libraries but within a library from one year to the next.

Further Possibilities

• Determine registration by user groups, such as children, young adults, and adults. This requires analyzing a sample of the registration records.
• Analyze registration by zip code to determine where users live with respect to the library. This also requires analyzing a sample of the registration records.

Materials Use Measures

A major library service is providing materials in a variety of formats for use inside and outside the library. The Materials Use Measures reflect the extent of use of the library's collection.

• **Circulation per Capita** represents the use of library materials outside the library. It measures circulation per person in the area served.

• **In-Library Materials Use per Capita** reflects the use of materials inside the library, per person in the area served.
• **Turnover Rate** measures the intensity of the use of the collection. It relates the circulation of materials to the size of the collection. It is the annual circulation per cataloged item held.

Circulation per Capita

Definition: Average annual circulation per person in the community served.

Calculation: ANNUAL CIRCULATION divided by POPULATION OF LEGAL SERVICE AREA.

Data Collection: Most libraries already count circulation.

ANNUAL CIRCULATION is the total circulation of all library materials of all types, including renewals.

Example: A library with a POPULATION OF LEGAL SERVICE AREA of 100,047 had an ANNUAL CIRCULATION of 1,030,484, for a **Circulation per Capita** of 10.3.

Analysis and Use of Data

• A high **Circulation per Capita** means heavy use of the circulating collection relative to the size of the community.
• Short loan periods may result in greater availability of materials and therefore higher **Circulation per Capita**.

• Short loan periods may also result in more renewals and therefore higher **Circulation per Capita**.
• A low **Circulation per Capita** may indicate a need to better match the collection to the community, or to do more to promote library services.
• A low **Circulation per Capita** and a high **Turnover Rate** may indicate a collection that is small relative to the size of the population served. It may also indicate problems with determining POPULATION OF LEGAL SERVICE AREA, or high use by people outside the legal service area.
• A low **Circulation per Capita** coupled with a

low **Turnover Rate** may indicate a library with a large noncirculating collection, many out-of-date materials, or a collection not well-matched to its users' interests.

- A high **Circulation per Capita** coupled with a low **Visits per Capita** means that fewer people borrow relatively more items on each visit; the same **Circulation per Capita** with a higher **Visits per Capita** means a smaller circulation per visit.
- A higher **Circulation per Capita** doesn't necessarily mean that more people use the library; it may simply mean that the people who use the library borrow more materials.

Possible approaches to increasing **Circulation per Capita**:

- Encourage library use by infrequent users or nonusers:

    Add outreach services
    Add materials to meet the needs of different populations.

- Increase use by those who already use the library:

    Analyze unfilled requests from the Materials

Availability Survey for areas in which the collection may be strengthened
Use merchandising techniques to promote the collection in the library.

- Shorten loan periods
- Add or change branch locations
- Add hours
- Add other forms of materials delivery, such as books by mail.

Collecting the Data

ANNUAL CIRCULATION is the total circulation of all library materials.

- Count all materials in all formats that are charged out for use outside the library
- Count renewals as circulations
- Interlibrary loan (ILL) transactions included are only items that you borrow for your users. Count them when your users take them home. Do not include loans to another library or branch.

Record on Data Elements Summary Sheet, Figure 26, item a.

Further Possibilities

- Determine **Circulation per Capita** separately for adults', young adults', and children's materials. This requires estimating the adult, young adult, and children's population, and recording adult, young adult, and children's circulation. (Not all children's materials circulate to children, and so forth; however, this gives a good approximation.)
- Calculate **Circulation per Capita** separately for various subjects or kinds of materials.
- Analyze a sample of circulation transactions to see how many items each borrower borrows. (See Sampling, under Data Collection, in Chapter 3.)
- Calculate what percentage of users account for 50 percent of the items borrowed. The smaller the percentage, the more that circulation is concentrated among a small group of users. A photocharge or automated circulation system is helpful for this.
- Determine what percentage of circulation is to nonresident users. Again, a photocharge or automated circulation system is useful, because you can look at the transaction records.

- Determine circulation per full-time equivalent (FTE) staff member.
- Measure circulation per hour that the library is open. This is especially useful for comparing branches, and other situations where POPULATION OF LEGAL SERVICE AREA is difficult to determine. Multiply the hours that a library is open per week by 52, and subtract the hours that the library is closed for holidays, to get Annual Hours Open. If hours vary by time of year, figure out how many weeks the library operates each schedule and how many total hours open this creates. Divide Annual Hours Open into ANNUAL CIRCULATION.
- Divide ANNUAL CIRCULATION by LIBRARY REGISTRATIONS to get Circulation per Registration.

Pointers/Special Considerations

Branches and multi-branch libraries may find it difficult to determine **Circulation per Capita** if the geographical boundaries of each community cannot be clearly established. (See Population of Legal Service Area, earlier in this chapter.)

In-Library Materials Use per Capita

Definition: Number of materials used in the library per person in the community served.

Calculation: ANNUAL IN-LIBRARY MATERIALS USE divided by POPULATION OF LEGAL SERVICE AREA.

Data Collection: Ask users not to reshelve, and for one week count all materials used.

Any item that is removed from the shelf (or from its usual location) by staff or public is considered "used." All formats of library materials are included. Just as circulation counts all items used outside the library, ANNUAL IN-LIBRARY MATERIALS USE counts all items used within the library. Each physical item (periodical issue or bound volume, microfilm reel, pamphlet file or folder, etc.) counts as one.

Example: During one sample week, 6703 items were used. 6703 × 52 = an ANNUAL IN-LIBRARY MATERIALS USE of 348,556. THE POPULATION OF LEGAL SERVICE AREA is 67,030. The **In-Library Materials Use per Capita** is 5.2 (388,556 divided by 67,080).

Analysis and Use of Data

Traditionally, libraries have used circulation data, and sometimes number of reference transactions, as indicators of activity levels. Adding **In-Library Materials Use per Capita** creates a more complete picture of service to the public, especially in libraries with extensive reference collections, or those where people tend to use materials in the library rather than checking them out.

- A high **In-Library Materials Use per Capita** may be associated with a high **Reference Transactions per Capita** and/or with a large reference collection.

• A high **In-Library Materials Use per Capita** may indicate that users tend to spend time in the library. It may indicate a need for a large seating capacity and/or for many copy machines, microfilm readers, and the like.

• A low **In-Library Materials Use per Capita** may indicate a library where people stop in to pick up materials to take home, and do not stay long.

Possible approaches to increasing **In-Library Materials Use per Capita** include:

• Make the library a more inviting place to spend time

• Increase the seating and study space

• Consider whether hours are convenient for people who would like to spend time in the library

• Add more seating geared to special groups, for example, different sizes of tables and chairs for children of different ages, or a homework corner for young adults.

Possible approaches to decreasing **In-Library Materials Use per Capita** are:

• Consider whether some reference materials should be made circulating

• Strengthen the circulating collection in subjects in which the reference collection is heavily used.

Collecting the Data

1. Choose a one-week "typical" period to collect data. See Scheduling section in Chapter 2.

2. Ask users not to reshelve their materials during this period. Post signs in obvious places throughout the library: "Survey in progress. Please do not reshelve materials."

   a. It may help to place booktrucks (or boxes, or laundry baskets, or whatever) throughout the library for people to leave materials on (or in). Label them prominently: "Please don't reshelve materials. Leave here." Arrange things so that it is easier for the user to leave the item than to reshelve it.

3. At least every hour on the hour throughout the sample days, collect and count materials left on tables or at collection points. Exclude those returned from outside circulation.

4. You can use the In-Library Materials Use Log, Figure 30, to collect the counts; use a separate log sheet for each day. You may

want separate log sheets in different parts of the library, for example, in different departments. (Figure 16 is a filled-out example.)

5. Enter the times when the counts are made across the top. If the library opens at 9:00 a.m., the first log entry would be for one hour later or 10:00 a.m., and so forth, until closing time.

6. Very busy libraries (or areas within a library) may need to collect materials more often. Simply add more columns to Figure 30.

7. The rows of Figure 30 are labelled by type of material. These categories are *suggestions* only: use whatever categories make sense in your library, or you may use only

Library _Main - Business Dept._

Date _10/4/86_

Use one tally sheet for each day. Every hour on the hour collect and count the materials left for reshelving. Enter the time at the top of the form.

Type of Material	Hour												Total
	10:00 am	11:00	12	1	2	3	4	5	6	7	8	9:00 pm	
Books	4	13	13	8	15	4	7	2	4	10	6	8	94
Magazines	18	24	33	28	35	8	13	1	6	18	20	10	214
Pamphlet Files													
Sound Recordings													
Newspapers	2	15	35	11	15	13	12	20	27	21	16	8	195
Controlled Materials[1]	0	13	7	15	0	12	20	0	4	0	0	0	71
Other _Reports_	5	15	7	3	13	4	8	27	3	0	3	0	88
Totals	29	80	95	65	78	41	60	50	44	49	45	26	662

[1] Desk reserve or other materials user has to check out for in-library use.

FIGURE 16 Worked Example of Figure 30: In-Library Materials Use Log

the total at the bottom and not count materials by type.

8. "Controlled Materials" on Figure 30 refers to materials that users must get from the staff, for example, books kept behind the reference desk. The staff responsible for those materials should have a copy of Figure 30 and count each item as it is given to the user.

9. Total the number of materials used during the entire sampling week. Multiply this total by 52 to get ANNUAL IN-LIBRARY MATERIALS USE. Record on Figure 26, Data Elements Summary Sheet, item b.

10. Divide by the POPULATION OF LEGAL SERVICE AREA (Data Elements Summary Sheet, Figure 26, item p) to determine **In-Library Materials Use per Capita**.

Pointers/Special Considerations

• An item is counted as used even if a patron looked at it and found that it wasn't what she or he wanted. Since not all circulating materials are read, this is consistent with **Circulation per Capita**.

• The counting process should not interfere with library operations. Delaying reshelving in popular areas may *decrease* use because people can't find what they need when they need it. In that case, collect and count materials more often.

- In some libraries, especially small libraries, users may be reluctant to leave materials "in the way." It helps to mark a spot (e.g., a book-truck) with a sign "Place materials here—please do not reshelve." This is also useful for users who want to protect their privacy—especially if the booktruck is not near a service desk.
- The use of some kinds of materials may be particularly challenging to measure without inconveniencing users. For example, put magazines in strict alphabetical order and check hourly.
- Some uses are almost impossible to count: for example, periodical indexes that are used continually. (Some libraries have put slips on each volume with a note asking people to make a mark every time they use it.) Other uses will go un-counted, for example, when a user looks at a book at the shelf and reshelves it. Do the best you can but know that no measure is perfect.
- It is easy to forget the collection time when staff are busy with other duties. Setting a timer or using an alarm clock will help.

Further Possibilities

- Determine **In-Library Materials Use per Capita** by type of material or subject area.
- Determine turnover rate based on in-library materials use (ANNUAL IN-LIBRARY MATE-RIALS USE divided by HOLDINGS). (See discussion of **Turnover Rate**, later in this chapter.)
- Analyze **In-Library Materials Use per Capita** by time of day.
- Conduct a user survey, asking people as they leave how many materials they used in the library. You can use a survey similar to the Materials Availability Survey, described later in this chapter.

Turnover Rate

Definition: Average circulation per volume owned.

Calculation: ANNUAL CIRCULATION divided by the library's HOLDINGS.

Data Collection: Use existing data, or estimate collection size by measuring shelflist.

ANNUAL CIRCULATION is the total circulation of all library materials for a year. For this measure, HOLDINGS is defined as the number of cataloged books, plus paperbacks and video-cassettes, even if uncataloged. Do not include periodicals, whether cataloged or not. Count physical items, not titles.

Example: The HOLDINGS of a library consist of 61,325 cataloged items and 6,000 uncataloged paperbacks for a total of 67,325 items. The ANNUAL CIRCULATION is 480,000. 480,000 divided by 67,325 = 7.13 **Turnover Rate**.

Analysis and Use of Data

- A high **Turnover Rate** means a high circulation compared to the collection size.
- A collection of mainly high-interest, circulating materials will have a high **Turnover Rate**.
- A library with a wide range of materials, in-cluding less popular titles, or with a large reference collection, will have a lower **Turnover Rate**.
- High **In-Library Materials Use** and a low **Turnover Rate** may mean that materials tend to be used inside rather than outside the library.
- A library with a large proportion of out-of-date or inappropriate materials will have a low **Turnover Rate**.
- High **Turnover** may result in a low **Materials Availability**, and vice versa: the more items off the shelf, the less likely a user is to find what she or he needs at the time.

Possibilities for increasing turnover:

- Weed the collection often
- Purchase multiple copies of popular materials, and discard them promptly as demand de-clines

- Make as many materials circulating as feasible
- Merchandise materials to attract user attention: e.g., displays of previous years' best sellers, displays tying in to popular movies and TV shows or current events
- Increase hours
- See also suggestions for increasing **Circulation per Capita**. Increasing circulation without increasing the collection size will increase **Turnover Rate**.

Collecting the Data

Most libraries already have the circulation and holdings data needed. If necessary, holdings can be estimated using one of the following methods.

1. *Physical Inventory.* Check the collection on the shelves and in circulation against the shelflist, and count the volumes owned and accounted for. Only feasible for small collections.

2. *Additions and Withdrawals.* If you have a beginning estimate of the size of the collection (e.g., from a past inventory), update it by subtracting withdrawals and adding additions since the last inventory.

3. *Automated Records.* A library with an automated circulation system often has a count of the items in the database. Add to the total materials not included in the database (e.g., noncirculating items).

4. *Measuring the Shelflist.* If there is a comprehensive shelflist for the collection to be measured (e.g., library, branch, etc.), the size of holdings can be approximated from the size of the shelflist, adjusting for multiple copies and adding in uncataloged items. Use Figure 31, Holdings Estimation Worksheet. Figure 17 is a worked example.

   a. Take ten one-inch samples from the shelflist.

		Cards per Inch	Vols. per Card
1. Take ten one-inch samples from the shelflist.	1a	80	b 1.4
	2a	15	b 1.6
For each sample count:	3a	82	b 1.8
	4a	74	b 1.1
(a) cards per inch	5a	84	b 1.4
	6a	65	b 2.1
(b) volumes[1] per card	7a	70	b 4.0
	8a	72	b 1.1
	9a	70	b 1.5
	10a	68	b 1.4
2. Average together the ten samples to get: (c) Average Number of Cards per Inch (d) Average Number of Volumes[1] per Card	2c	74	d 1.74
3. Measure the entire shelflist for Total Shelflist Inches.	3	1800	
4. Multiply the Average Number of Cards per Inch (2c) by the Total Shelflist Inches (3) = Estimated Number of Cards in Shelflist.	4	133,200	
5. Multiply the Average Number of Volumes per Card (2d) by Estimated Number of Cards in Shelflist (4). Result is Estimated Number of Volumes in Shelflist.	5	231,768	
6. Enter number of items for any materials not included in the shelflist.[2]	6	500	
7. Add (5) + (6) for Total Library HOLDINGS.	7	232,268	

[1] For nonprint items, count number of items (i.e., multiple copies). See text. [2] See definition of HOLDINGS in text.

FIGURE 17 Worked Example of Figure 31: Holdings Estimation Worksheet

1) Count the number of drawers in the shelflist and divide by 10. For example, if there are 125 drawers, the result is 12.5. Round this *down* to 12. Then pick every 12th drawer (numbers 12, 24, 36, etc.) until you have ten.

2) For each drawer, straighten the cards and push them to the front of the drawer; lay a ruler across the top; and remove a one-inch stack of cards from the middle of the drawer. Repeat until you have ten one-inch stacks from ten different drawers.

b. For each of the one-inch samples, count:

1) The number of cards (line 1, column a, of Figure 31).

2) The number of volumes represented by the cards in that inch (line 1, column b). For example, you may have multiple copies of some titles, and others may be multi-volume sets.

c. Average together the ten samples to get:

1) Average number of cards per inch (line 2c)

2) Average number of volumes per card (line 2d)

d. Now measure the entire shelflist by compressing the cards in each drawer and using a ruler to measure the number of inches of cards in each drawer. The total for all drawers added together is the total shelflist inches (line 3).

e. Follow the directions on lines 4 through 7 of Figure 31, the Holdings Estimation Worksheet, to estimate your holdings from this information.

f. Be sure you add in any cataloged materials not included in the book shelflist (line 6). Measure special format materials represented in their own shelflists (e.g., video-cassettes) separately and use a copy of Figure 31 to estimate the number of these items; then add them to the results for other formats.

g. The result is an approximation of HOLDINGS (Figure 26, Data Elements Summary Sheet, item f).

Pointers/Special Considerations

- HOLDINGS figures that are not corrected for materials withdrawn, lost in circulation, etc., will be inflated and the **Turnover Rate** will be lower.
- **Turnover Rate** is sensitive to the relative sizes of the circulating and noncirculating collections.
- HOLDINGS includes both circulating and noncirculating materials because of the variety of library policies concerning what does and does not circulate.

Further Possibilities

- Compute a new turnover rate for the circulating collection only.
- Compute separate turnover rates by subject. This is most feasible where the circulation system is automated. The holdings measurement methods described above can all be done by subject.
- Compute separate turnover rates by type of material such as books, sound recordings, magazines. Count each physical unit as one (e.g., periodical volume, microfilm reel, microfiche card, etc.).
- Compute a second turnover rate that includes both circulation and in-library materials use. This is especially useful for collections with large numbers of noncirculating materials and a high level of in-library use.
- Compute in-library turnover (in-library materials use divided by holdings) for noncirculating collections like microforms.

Materials Access Measures

Like the Materials Use Measures, the Materials Access Measures are concerned with the use of the library's collection. The Materials Use Measures are concerned with the extent of use of the collection. The Materials Access Measures reflect users' success in obtaining the materials they want.

- The Materials Availability Measures are a subset of the Materials Access Measures. They reflect users' success in finding what they are looking for during their visit.

  Title Fill Rate is the proportion of specific titles sought that were found during the user's visit.

Subject and Author Fill Rate is the proportion of searches for materials on a subject or by an author that were successful during the visit.

Browsers' Fill Rate is the proportion of users who were browsing, rather than looking for something specific, who found something useful.

• **Document Delivery** is a second kind of Materials Access Measure. When users cannot get what they need immediately, they may ask the library to borrow or reserve materials for them. **Document Delivery** measures how long a user waits for these materials, including reserves and interlibrary loans.

Materials Availability Measures

Definition: Proportion of title and subject/author searches and of people browsing that are successful.

Calculation: Number of successful searches divided by all searches, for each type of search.

Data Collection: Materials Availability Survey, a survey of library users.

• **Title Fill Rate**
• **Subject and Author Fill Rate**
• **Browsers' Fill Rate**

These three measures reflect the degree to which library users were able to get the materials they were looking for during their visit. All three use data from the Materials Availability Survey (instructions below).

• **Title Fill Rate**

The percentage of specific titles sought that were found in the library at the time of the request, including those requested by telephone.
Calculation: NUMBER OF TITLES FOUND divided by NUMBER OF TITLES SOUGHT.
Example: A user searching for *Dinner at the Homesick Restaurant* reports one title sought. If the user finds the book, that is one title found. One user may report more than one title sought.

• **Subject and Author Fill Rate**

The percentage of requests for materials on a given subject or by a specific author found at the time of the request. A request is considered "filled" if the user reports that she or he found something.
Calculation: NUMBER OF SUBJECTS AND AUTHORS FOUND divided by NUMBER OF SUBJECTS AND AUTHORS SOUGHT.

Example: anything by Ann Tyler; a book about restaurant management. Again, one user may report more than one search.

• **Browsers' Fill Rate**

The percentage of users looking casually for something interesting (not for a specific title, subject, or author) who found something.
Calculation: NUMBER OF BROWSERS FINDING SOMETHING divided by NUMBER OF BROWSERS.
Example: Someone who comes in looking for "something good to read" is a browser.

Title and **Subject and Author Fill Rates** are the proportion of searches that are successful, not the proportion of users who were satisfied. A user may search for more than one title and/or subject on one visit. **Browsers' Fill Rate**, however, is the proportion of users who were satisfied.

Example: During the sample period, one library counted 377 TITLES SOUGHT and 220 TITLES FOUND, for a **Title Fill Rate** of 58 percent (220/377). They counted 482 SUBJECTS AND AUTHORS SOUGHT and 287 SUBJECTS AND AUTHORS FOUND, for a **Subject and Author Fill Rate** of 60 percent (287/482). In addition, 280 users reported that they were BROWSERS, of whom 227 found something, for a **Browsers' Fill Rate** of 81 percent (227/280).

Analysis and Use of Data

Another way of looking at the **Fill Rates** is that each represents the probability that a search will be successful. A 60 percent **Title Fill Rate** means that the average user has a 60 percent chance of finding the title she or he is looking for.

The **Fill Rates** may reflect several things:

- The match between the library's collection and the users' wants
- The extent to which materials are owned and on the shelf when someone wants them
- How well users find things in the library.

The **Fill Rates** do not tell the library whether unsuccessful searches are due to the collection, the library's policies and procedures (longer loan periods may make it less likely that what people want will be on the shelf), or the user (such as users' ability to find materials on their own).

It is very important that these measures be looked at in the context of other measures, especially the Materials Use Measures: **Turnover Rate** and **Circulation per Capita**. The Materials Availability Measures indicate how successful users are, but not how much the library is used. If a library is rarely used, then the visitor's chance of finding materials on the shelf is quite high. When a library is very busy, however, some users are inevitably disappointed when what they are looking for is currently being used by someone else. The highest **Fill Rates** of all might occur in a library with a totally noncirculating collection.

A library with a low **Circulation per Capita** and/or a low **Turnover Rate** may have high **Fill Rates** because the collection is not being used. If a library increases its **Circulation per Capita** but not its **Fill Rates** from one year to the next, it is probably providing its users with more service. Although the **Fill Rates** haven't changed, the community is using the collection more and therefore getting more benefit from its library.

Other relationships to consider include:

- A high **Reference Transactions per Capita** and low **Subject and Author Fill Rate** may indicate that users are having trouble finding subject materials on their own and asking for help.
- A library with low **Fill Rates** and high **Circulation per Capita** may be exceptionally busy.

Generally, **Title Fill Rate** will be lower than **Subject and Author Fill Rate** because the library has more alternatives for filling subject/author requests. **Browsers' Fill Rate** is usually the highest of all.

Low **Fill Rates** may mean frustrated users. Ways to increase **Fill Rates** are:

- Examine your collection, especially in more popular areas, to see if you need to add titles, buy more duplicates, or shift purchasing from one area to another
- Speed up the reshelving of high-use materials
- Make it easier for users to find materials in the catalog and on the shelves
- Examine reserve, interlibrary loan, and reference requests to identify areas in which the collection needs improvement
- Shorten the circulation period for high-use materials
- Examine the responses to the Materials Availability Survey for ideas on ways to improve the collection.

Very high **Fill Rates** could indicate an underutilized collection. People have little trouble finding what they are looking for because materials aren't circulating, or because people are tailoring their searches to what they expect to find in the library. Possible ways to reduce **Fill Rates** include:

- Promote the library and its collection, inside and outside the library. Increasing **Circulation per Capita** may reduce the Fill Rates.
- Publicize the availability of reserves and interlibrary loan. Let people know that the library can get for them materials not on the shelf. This may encourage people to look for materials that they might not have expected the library to provide.

Collecting the Data

The data for these measures come from the Materials Availability Survey and a count of telephone requests, instructions for both of which follow. The Materials Availability Survey consists of giving a questionnaire to each person using the library during specified time periods, asking them to list what they looked for and whether or not they found it. The Telephone Request Tally adds in requests made over the telephone.

Pointers/Special Considerations

- Small libraries and others where most use is browsing may have difficulty collecting enough title and subject and author searches for a reasonable sample. For them **Browsers' Fill Rate** may be the most appropriate **Fill Rate**. Generally, a library needs to be able to collect at least 100 searches within two weeks to be able to use the associated measure.

- It is very difficult for users to distinguish between reference transactions (discussed later in this chapter) and Subject and Author Searches. In the interests of simplicity, the Materials Availability Survey does not tackle the problem of distinguishing between these two. This means that some reference transactions will be included in calculating the **Subject and Author Fill Rate**.
- Because these measures are calculated from samples, they are estimates.

  The library's "true" **Fill Rates** may be a few percentage points lower or higher. Small differences among libraries or over time may be due to fluctuations in the measures rather than changes in library performance. See Sampling, under Data Collection, in Chapter 3.

  Analysis of user's written comments and/or of the subject areas of failed searches may be particularly useful for diagnosing slight changes in service levels over time.

- **Fill Rates** depend not only on the library but also on users, including the variety of their requests and how adept they are at using the library. Differences in user communities should be considered in comparing **Fill Rates** across libraries and branches.

Further Possibilities

- Calculate separate children's, young adult, and adult **Title** and **Subject and Author Fill Rates** (ask age on the survey form). (Note that this would reflect each group's success in finding what they want, not people's success in finding children's, young adults', and adults' materials.)
- Follow up on materials not found to see why they weren't found. Were they not owned, owned but not available, available but not found by the user? This requires that the staff collect the forms quickly and trace the materials. See, for example, Paul B. Kantor, "Availability Analysis," *Journal of the American Society for Information Science* 27 (October 1976): 311–19.
- Analyze **Title** and **Subject and Author Fill Rates** by subject area.
- Read through the Materials Availability Survey responses and categorize the unfilled requests. Use this information for collection development.

Materials Availability Survey

Supplies Needed to Conduct Survey

Adequate copies of the MAS form (Figure 33).

Pencils for users to borrow.

Sealed boxes for returning survey forms.

Signs for all entrances to library. Suggested text:
LIBRARY SURVEY TODAY. YOUR COOPERATION IS APPRECIATED.

Signs for all exits and the circulation desk. Suggested text:
HAVE YOU RETURNED YOUR SURVEY FORM? THANK YOU.

Copies of the Materials Availability Fact Sheet (Figure 34) for everyone administering the survey and library service desks.

The Materials Availability Survey (MAS) is used to collect the data for the Materials Availability Measures: **Title Fill Rate**, **Subject and Author Fill Rate**, and **Browsers' Fill Rate**. The Materials Availability Survey asks users how successful they were during their current library visit at finding specific titles, at finding materials by an author or on a subject, and at browsing. At the same time, staff are tallying telephone requests to get a total view of user success.

This section provides step-by-step directions for scheduling and administering the Materials Availability Survey, keeping the Telephone Request Tally, and calculating the Materials Availability Measures.

Scheduling the Materials Availability Survey

Several decisions have to be made when scheduling the Materials Availability Survey (MAS):

• When during the year to do the MAS
• What goals to set for the numbers of questionnaires handed out and collected, and of searches reported: these determine for how long a period of time the survey must be performed
• What days of the week and times of day during the sample period to administer the survey.

WHEN TO DO THE MAS

1. Select a "typical" period when nothing unusual is happening that would affect library activities. See Scheduling section in Chapter 2.
2. If you are also collecting data for **Reference Transactions per Capita** and/or **Reference Completion Rate**, you may or may not want to do the MAS at the same time.

   a. Both the MAS and the Reference Services Measures require the reference staff to keep tallies. It may confuse them to tally telephone requests for materials for the MAS and reference transactions for the Reference Services Measures at the same time.
   b. On the other hand, it is possible to modify the Reference Tally Sheet (Figure 40) to incorporate the Telephone Request Tally Form (Figure 35). This would avoid possible confusion over how to count telephone requests for materials while tally-.ing reference transactions (requests for materials are not included in reference transactions).

HOW MANY QUESTIONNAIRES

The number of questionnaires to be handed out depends on how many questionnaires are needed to reach the target sample size of searches for the **Fill Rates**.

Example: A library distributed 1,000 MAS Forms to users. 690 were returned with usable responses for a response rate of 69 percent. (The remainder were never returned, or were unreadable.) Of the questionnaires returned, 30% reported one or more titles sought. (The rest reported no title searches.) 377 total TITLES SOUGHT were reported.

Figure 32, Calculating the MAS Sample, can be used to determine how many questionnaires to distribute and how long it will take. Figure 18 is a worked example.

1. Begin by determining your target number of

TITLES SOUGHT. Enter on line 1 of Figure 32.

   a. Because most libraries' users report fewer TITLES SOUGHT than SUBJECTS AND AUTHORS SOUGHT or BROWSING VISITS, a survey with enough TITLES SOUGHT will probably have enough responses for the other measures, too.
   b. To determine your target number of TITLES SOUGHT, either calculate your own sample size for **Title Fill Rate** or use the recommended sample size: preferably 400, but at least 100 (see Sampling, under Data Collection, in Chapter 3, to determine your sample size).

      1) A library that cannot get at least 100 TITLES SOUGHT and 100 SUBJECTS AND AUTHORS SOUGHT within two weeks should not use the Materials Availability Measures, or it should use *only* **Browsers' Fill Rate**. Many small libraries are used primarily for browsing, and so **Browsers' Fill Rate** is the most applicable of the Materials Availability Measures. In that case, the library needs at least 100 people checking the "browsing" question on the materials availability questionnaire within two weeks. While it may be useful for the staff to read through the answers to the other questions, the results for **Title** and **Subject and Author Fill Rates** probably won't be sufficiently accurate (see Sampling, under Data Collection, in Chapter 3).

2. Enter on line 2 the average number of title searches that you expect on each questionnaire. This information can come from any of the following:

   a. The recommended MAS Pretest (described below)
   b. Your library's past experience, if you have done the MAS before
   c. A default assumption of .6 title searches per questionnaire returned. Note that this is based on other libraries' experiences: yours may be different.

3. Line 3 calculates the number of questionnaires that must be returned to get the required number of title searches.
4. Not all questionnaires come back, and not everyone follows instructions. The number of questionnaires to hand out (line 5) depends on the proportion of usable responses

	Your Library OR	Default[1]
1. Desired number of title requests[2]	*200*	400
2. Title requests per questionnaire	*.5*	.6
3. Target number of questionnaires (line 1 divided by line 2)	*400*	670
4. Response rate	*.8*	.7
5. Number of questionnaires to hand out (line 3 divided by line 4)	*500*	960
6. Expected questionnaires distributed per hour	*20*	[3]
7. Number of hours to distribute questionnaires (line 5 divided by line 6)	*25*	

[1] If data are lacking for an individual library, use these recommendations.
[2] Since most libraries receive fewer title requests than subject or browsing searches, basing the sample size on titles ensures an adequate size for all three.
[3] Use your own library's data on visits, circulation, whatever is available.

FIGURE 18 Worked Example of Figure 32: Calculating the Materials Availability Survey Sample

you expect to get back, that is, the response rate (line 4). This figure can come from the MAS Pretest or your library's past experience, where applicable. The default figure for line 4 is 70 percent.

5. The length of time needed to distribute the target number of questionnaires on line 5 of Figure 32 depends on how many people use your library. You can determine this from the MAS Pretest or your past experience, or from whatever data you have on your library's use, such as number of visits per day or per hour (perhaps collected for **Library Visits per Capita**, or using a turnstile counter) or from your circulation figures. No default figure can be recommended.

   Example: Using the default values for Figure 32, a library that needs 400 TITLES SOUGHT must get back 670 questionnaires (rounded up from 666). Given a response rate of 70 percent, it must hand out 960. This library expects to distribute 75 questionnaires per hour. It needs to administer the survey over 15 hours.

For simplicity, telephone requests are left out of these calculations.

All of these calculations are best done using your library's data rather than the default values. The MAS Pretest (described below) is useful for developing this information.

WHEN TO HAND OUT QUESTIONNAIRES

1. The number of hours during which a library distibutes MAS questionnaires was determined above using Figure 32.
2. The goal is to schedule the survey hours so that all the days of the week and times of day that the library is open are represented.

   • If a library were to simply start collecting questionnaires on Monday morning, for example, and stop when it reached its goal, it might be finished by Wednesday. If the people who use the library at the end of the week and on the weekend are looking for different kinds of materials from those at the beginning of the week (e.g., the homework crush comes Wednesday nights; the weekend home-repair crowd comes in on Saturday), the results will not represent all the kinds of uses that people make of the library.

3. The MAS should be distributed over the days of week and time periods that the library is

open roughly in proportion to the library's schedule.

Example: A library is open 60 hours a week, including:

- 4 weekday mornings from 9 to 12, for a total of 12 morning hours, or 20 percent of its schedule
- 5 weekday afternoons from 12 to 5, or 25 afternoon hours, 42 percent of its schedule
- 4 weekday evenings from 5 to 9, for 16 evening hours, 25 percent of the total hours open
- 8 hours on Saturday, 13 percent of the total.

This library's MAS is to run for at least 15 hours. Multiplying 15 by the percent of the hours open that each period of time accounts for, the MAS should run for 3 morning hours (20% of 15), 6 afternoon hours (42% of 15), 4 evening hours, and 2 hours on Saturday, for a total of 15 hours. The MAS is scheduled over the week as shown in Figure 19.

There is no "formula" to this schedule: the hours were distributed to try to get an overall representation of days and hours that the library is open, avoiding the least busy periods (when few questionnaires could be collected). Some libraries have found that two-hour blocks work well for staffing.

This schedule is for a very busy library. Most libraries will distribute the survey times over two weeks, rather than one. In doing so, be sure that the schedules for the two weeks complement one another: for example, collect data on Tuesday morning one week, Tuesday afternoon the next.

Note that questionnaires are handed out to everyone *entering* the library during these periods. They will return the questionnaires when they leave, which may be after you have stopped distributing questionnaires for the day.

Time of Day	Mon.	Tues.	Wed.	Thur.	Fri.	Sat.	Sun.
9–10		SURVEY					
10–11					SURVEY		
11–12					SURVEY		
12–1				SURVEY		SURVEY	
1–2				SURVEY		SURVEY	
2–3			SURVEY				
3–4	SURVEY		SURVEY				
4–5	SURVEY						
5–6		SURVEY					
6–7		SURVEY					
7–8				SURVEY			
8–9				SURVEY			

- = an hour the library is open
- SURVEY = an hour during which the MAS is conducted
- = an hour the library is closed

FIGURE 19 Sample Materials Availability Survey Schedule

Administering the Materials Availability Survey

STAFFING AND TRAINING

Select a survey coordinator responsible for materials, procedures, training, problem-solving, data analysis, and so forth. Generally, this will be the data coordinator.

The people handing out forms may be either staff members or volunteers. In some libraries, users respond better to people they can identify as staff members: but they may also ask the staff for help, directions, etc., that may interfere with the survey process. It helps if surveyors are easily identified as part of the library: a name tag or badge, for example. Some users are more willing to cooperate if they know that the library is doing the survey.

Surveyors need to be well-trained to ensure that they approach users in a friendly and nonthreatening way, can answer users' questions, and will politely but firmly ask people to turn in MAS forms as they leave. It helps to have some practice sessions for them to rehearse.

All staff members, regardless of whether they are directly involved in the MAS, should know the basics about the survey. People may ask them questions. Staff can answer questions about the form but must not influence people's responses in any way. The Materials Availability Fact Sheet (Figure 34) will help them answer questions. Each person helping to conduct the survey should have a copy of the fact sheet. Additional copies for library staff members should be at all the service desks.

PRETEST THE MAS

Every new procedure has its problems. It is highly recommended that you do a short pretest before doing the MAS for the first time. The pretest is a one- or two-hour "rehearsal" of the MAS, best done during a moderately busy period. It is conducted exactly like the MAS itself, but the questionnaires are not tabulated as part of the full-scale MAS. The pretest serves two functions:

1. A test of all the procedures. A dry run can help the library to spot possible problems and fine-tune its training and procedures before the survey actually begins.
2. The pretest results can provide estimates of the response rate and the number of searches reported on each questionnaire, to be used in Figure 32 (lines 2 and 4).

THE MATERIALS AVAILABILITY SURVEY

1. Duplicate an ample number of MAS Survey forms (Figure 33). If a large part of your clientele speaks a language other than English, you should translate this form into their language(s) as well. (This requires tabulators who can read these responses, too.)
2. Number the Materials Availability Survey forms (a number stamping machine helps) so that you will know how many were given out and how many came back, and so that during tabulation you can check back to the original form if questions arise.
3. During the sample periods, every user entering the library gets a form—no exceptions! Including children. All entrances must be covered.
4. If many of your clients have poor reading skills, or may otherwise have problems filling out the questionnaire, have additional staff available to help them. Children may need help, as well.
5. Users should fill out the questionnaire just before they leave the library, not as they enter.
6. Forms are collected at the exit.

    a. Have sealed boxes for the forms near all the exits, and at the Circulation Desk. Sealed boxes help to protect users' privacy, especially in small libraries.
    b. Someone should be at the exit reminding people to turn in their questionnaires. This can be the same person handing them out if the library is not too busy.

7. It is important that *everyone* returns a form. *The demeanor of the person collecting forms (and handing them out) can affect the number of forms that come back.* Because the response rate can affect the results, this is extremely important. Be assertive and friendly, not aggressive. This is no place for a shy person.

    a. All users who refuse to participate should be counted. Either (1) the surveyor marks a questionnaire "refused" and drops it in the return box, or (2) surveyors keep tallies of refusals. Decide ahead of time which method is most appropriate for your library and pick one.

The MAS can also be administered as an interview rather than a self-administered questionnaire (see Surveys section of Data Sources, under Data Collection, in Chapter 3).

Use one tally form for each day

Library *Main – Science Dept.*

Date *10 / 8 / 86*

10 am – noon

TITLE REQUESTS:

On shelf	Not on shelf
ЦНТ ЦНТ II	ЦНТ III
TOTAL: *12*	TOTAL: *8*

SUBJECT AND AUTHOR REQUESTS:

On shelf	Not on shelf
ЦНТ ЦНТ	IIII
TOTAL: *10*	TOTAL: *4*

Count all telephone calls asking whether specific materials (specific books, issues of magazines, film titles, etc.) are currently available. Count as "on shelf" materials that you find on the shelf, that the user could pick up immediately. Count as "not on shelf" materials that are not owned, on order, out in circulation, or otherwise currently unavailable.

FIGURE 20   Worked Example of Figure 35: Telephone Request Tally Form

Telephone Request Tally

During the same time periods that you administer the Materials Availability Survey, tally all the telephone requests for materials using Figure 35, Telephone Request Tally Form. (Figure 20 is a worked example.) *Don't* tally requests all day long, only during the MAS sampling periods.

1. Use a separate tally sheet for each sampling period (e.g., Monday morning, Tuesday afternoon, etc.).
2. You will need a form at each phone where

such requests are received: for example, in a large library with subject departments you may need one at each department's reference desk.

3. Tally each request as either positive (item is currently available) or negative (item is not currently available, that is, not owned, not on the shelf, etc.).
4. At the end of the sampling period, gather all the tally forms and total the results.
5. These are added to the results of the MAS using Figure 37, Materials Availability Survey Summary.

Tabulation

The MAS forms should be tabulated by staff members who are fairly well-acquainted with the library and the kinds of things that people are looking for. People don't always follow directions, so the staff should be able to recognize common titles and to distinguish between title and subject searches. In most libraries, this would be high-level support staff or professional staff.

If some questionnaires have been distributed in a language other than English, someone who knows this language is needed to tabulate these.

1. Use the Materials Availability Survey Tabulation Form, Figure 36. (Figure 21 is a worked example.) You will need enough copies to record all the survey forms that you handed out. Enter the number of each survey form in the first column.

2. A person may report one or more title and/or subject searches and browse on the same visit; he or she may do some but not all of these searches; or he or she may do none of these.

3. *Titles:* For each survey form, on the line of the tabulation form with the survey form number, record the number of titles sought in column 1a, and the number found in 1b.

   a. A title search is a search for a specific item. It need not be a book, but may be

Form Number	(1) Title (a) Number Sought	(1) Title (b) Number Found	(2) Subject/Author (a) Number Sought	(2) Subject/Author (b) Number Found	(3) Browsing (a) Browsers	(3) Browsing (b) Found Something	(4) Other (a) Other	(4) Other (b) Refused, Blank, or Missing
1	1	1	0	0	0	0	0	0
2	0	0	3	2	0	0	0	0
3	0	0	0	0	1	1	0	0
4	0	0	0	0	0	0	1	0
5	0	0	0	0	0	0	0	1
6	5	4	1	0	0	0	0	0
7	4	2	1	1	0	0	0	0
8	2	0	1	1	0	0	0	0
9	0	0	2	2	0	0	0	0
10	0	0	0	0	1	1	0	0
11	2	1	2	2	0	0	0	0
12	0	0	0	0	1	0	0	0
TOTAL	14	8	10	8	3	2	1	1
Enter on Figure 37	line 7	line 10	line 13	line 16	line 19	line 20	line 3	line 5
	TITLES SOUGHT	TITLES FOUND	SUBJECTS/ AUTHORS SOUGHT	SUBJECTS/ AUTHORS FOUND	NUMBER OF BROWSERS	BROWSERS FINDING SOMETHING	OTHER	NOT USABLE

FIGURE 21 Worked Example of Figure 36: Materials Availability Survey Tabulation Form

a specific magazine (e.g., "current issue of *Time*"), movie, etc.

4. *Subjects or Authors:* Record the number of subjects and authors sought in column 2a, and the number found in column 2b.

 a. A subject/author search is a search for material on a subject or by an author.

 1) Include searches for particular genres of fiction (e.g., science fiction, romances).
 2) Do not count as subject searches the following responses: "novels" or "fiction" (unspecified); "new books"; type of material (e.g., magazines, movies); "nonfiction." If the user has listed one of these kinds of searches, this is considered a browsing search. Code and count the search as browsing.

5. *Browsing:* If the question about browsing was answered, put a "1" in column 3(a) "Browser."

 a. If the answer to the browsing question is "Yes," also put a "1" in column 3(b).
 b. If the answer is "no," enter a zero.
 c. If the browsing question was not checked, put zeros in both 3(a) and 3(b).

6. *Other:* If the user checked *only* the "Other" question, put a "1" in column 4(a) and zeroes in all others. (The point of the "other" question is to allow all users to return a form, and to avoid confusion among users who did not search for materials.)

 a. If they marked the "Other" question but also answered elsewhere, ignore the answer to the "Other" question.

7. Do *not* count (in either the "Sought" or "Found" columns) searches for which the user did not indicate whether the material was found. Counting these in the "Sought" column but not the "Found" column would erroneously treat them as failed searches, reducing the library's fill rate.

8. Any search for which the user's response is unclear or incomplete should not be counted at all. (On the questionnaire, write in red next to the answer "NC" for "not coded.") If the questionnaire is not codable (no questions were legibly answered, or the questionnaire is marked "refused" or is blank), put a "1" in column 4(b) and zeroes in all other columns.

9. In some cases, users may have clearly confused subject and title searches, or not followed directions. You may *correct* such clear mistakes, but *with caution:* only the user knows what she or he was looking for. *The coder is not to overrule the user except in clear cases. When in doubt, the user is right.*

 a. Mark on the questionnaire in red any changes or interpretations that you make. For example, if the user has not marked the browsing question, but has listed under subject/author searches "novels," line through in red the answer under subjects, and check in red the browsing question. This is so that if you need to go back to the questionnaires you know how each question was coded.

10. Total the columns on each sheet, and add together the totals from all the MAS Tabulation Forms.

11. Turn to Figure 37, Materials Availability Survey Summary, and follow the instructions on the form. It tells how to add together the results from Figure 35, Telephone Request Tally, and Figure 36, Materials Availability Survey Tabulation, to get your library's **Title**, **Subject and Author**, and **Browsers' Fill Rates**. (Figure 22 is a worked example.)

 a. Only the "unavailable" or "not on shelf" responses on the telephone tally are counted; presumably titles that were available were picked up later by the user and counted then.

12. All these measures need to be expressed as confidence intervals. See Confidence Intervals, in the Sampling section under Data Collection in Chapter 3 for instructions on how to calculate.

The section Libraries with Multiple Outlets under Data Analysis in Chapter 3 tells you how to calculate library-level Materials Availability Measures.

If too few of the people surveyed participate, the results may not be representative. A low participation rate on a survey usually means that there is something wrong with the survey: the questionnaire is too difficult, or the questions asked don't apply to the users, or the staff handing out and collecting the forms are not persuasive enough. Generally, a library should have

Response Rate	
1. Number of questionnaires handed out	400
2. Questionnaires returned with usable title, subject and author, or browsing answers (total questionnaires minus the total of columns 4a and 4b, Figure 36)	300
3. Questionnaires with *only* "Other" question checked (total of column 4a, Figure 36)	10
4. Usable questionnaires (subtotal lines (2) + (3))	310
5. Questionnaires marked "refused," with no usable responses, or never returned (total of column 4b, Figure 36)	90
6. Response rate (line (4) divided by line (1))	78%

Title Fill Rate		
7. TITLES SOUGHT (total of column 1a, Figure 36)		350
8. Titles not available (Telephone Request Tally Form, Figure 35)		27
9. Total TITLES SOUGHT (line (7) + line (8))		377
10. TITLES FOUND (total of column 1b, Figure 36)		220
11. **Title Fill Rate** (line (10) divided by line (9))		58%
12. Confidence interval for **Title Fill Rate** (See Figure 6)	LOW:	55%
	HIGH:	61%

FIGURE 22 Worked Example of Figure 37: Materials Availability Survey Summary

Subject Fill Rate	
13. SUBJECTS AND AUTHORS SOUGHT (total of column, 2a, Figure 36)	470
14. Subjects and Authors not available (Telephone Request Tally Form, Figure 35)	12
15. Total SUBJECTS AND AUTHORS SOUGHT (line (13) + line (14))	482
16. SUBJECTS AND AUTHORS FOUND (total of column 2b, Figure 36)	287
17. **Subject and Author Fill Rate** (line (16) divided by line (15))	60%
18. Confidence interval for **Subject and Author Fill Rate** (see Figure 6) LOW:	56%
HIGH:	64%

Browsers' Fill Rate	
19. NUMBER OF BROWSERS (total of column 3a, Figure 36)	280
20. NUMBER OF BROWSERS FINDING SOMETHING (total of column 3b, Figure 36)	227
21. **Browsers' Fill Rate** (line (20) divided by line (19))	81%
22. Confidence interval for **Browsers' Fill Rate** (see Figure 6) LOW:	78%
HIGH:	84%

FIGURE 22 Worked Example of Figure 37: Materials Availability Survey Summary (continued)

a response rate of at least 60 percent for the results to be meaningful. Use Figure 37 to calculate the response rate.

Example: A library distributed 400 Materials Availability Survey forms. 300 of them were returned with responses that could be coded using Figure 36. Another 10 users answered the "Other" question, indicating that they had not come to the library looking for materials. Therefore a total of 310 people answered the questionnaire and followed instructions. Another 20 questionnaires were unintelligible, 5 had been marked "refused" by the staff distributing questionnaires, and 65 questionnaires just never turned up—apparently users had thrown them away or taken them home. The library's response rate is 78 percent (310 divided by 400).

Document Delivery

Definition: Percent of requested materials available within 7, 14, and 30 days, and longer.

Calculation: Determine the percent of requests being tracked that are filled within 7, 14, and 30 days, or longer.

Data Collection: Track one month's worth of requests for up to 30 days after they are placed.

Document Delivery measures the number of days required to get to users those materials not available at the time of their visits, either because the materials are not owned by the library, or because they are owned but are being used by someone else. Most libraries cannot have immediately available all the materials that their users request. This measure reflects how rapidly the library fills these requests.

Example: A library tracked one month's worth of requests, for a total of 299. Of these, 72 (24%) were filled within 7 days, 20 percent between 8 and 14 days, 33 percent in 15 to 30 days, and 22 percent in more than 30 days.

Figure 38 is a log to be used in tracking requests. The source codes in Figure 38 are suggested only: use the breakdown that makes the most sense for your library. Figure 38 categorizes sources into:

- Reserves: materials owned but temporarily unavailable (code R)
- External ILLs: materials borrowed from another library (code I)
- Internal ILLs: materials borrowed from another branch of the same library (regardless of whether the requesting library owns the item) (code B)
- Purchases: items not owned when requested but subsequently bought in response to the user's request, or items on order when the user requests them (code O)

- Other (code X).

Time counted is from the day the material is requested to the day it is physically available for borrowing, regardless of when the user picks it up.

Comparisons across libraries are best made using the results for all types of requests taken together (the bottom or "ALL" line of Figure 39).

Analysis and Use of Data

Document Delivery measures how long users have to wait for requests. If **Document Delivery** is slower than you would like, you may want to study the various components of document delivery to determine which aspect(s) need(s) attention. Some possible ways to reduce the wait:

- Consider whether your library is borrowing through ILL titles that it should own
- Buy more copies of high demand titles
- Make your ordering or processing more efficient
- Arrange for more frequent delivery between branches
- Improve your interlibrary and/or intralibrary loan procedures and/or delivery
- Change your library's policies about when you buy and when you borrow an item that is not owned
- Establish rush processing for urgent requests
- Consider buying heavily demanded titles locally rather than through your usual acquisitions process.

Collecting the Data

At least one month's worth of requests (i.e., all the requests placed by users over a period of one month) are needed. More requests will give a more precise estimate. These should total at least 100 requests. A library that handles fewer than 100 requests per month should probably record all requests for the entire year, or record requests over several periods during the year to a total of 100.

1. Pick a beginning day during a "typical" period (see Scheduling section in Chapter 2). Using Figure 38, Document Delivery Log, record every request during the next month. (Figure 23 is a filled-in example.)
2. Requests should be logged where the user

Library _Main_

Date Begun _9/1/86_

Date Ended _9/30/86_

Request No.	ID for Item	Date Requested Month/Day	Date Available Month/Day	Response Time (days)	Code[1]
1	Birnham, J. Birnham's Theory	9/4	10/22	47	R
2	Onosko, Commodore 64	9/4	patron cancelled		
3	Angelou, All God's...	9/2	10/7	34	R
4	Beachley, Q Clearance	9/4	10/17	42	O
5	Crane, Legacy of Lady Smith	9/4	10/7	32	I
6	Galsworthy, End of the Chapter	9/4	9/15	11	O
7	Gardner, Case of the Restless...	9/4	9/7	3	R
8	Gardner, Case of Runaway...	9/4	10/9	35	I
9	Naipaul, Bend in the River	9/4	9/18	14	O
10	Perter, Curse of Pharaohs	9/5	9/20	15	B
11	Seth, Golden Gate	9/5	9/23	17	B
12	Andrews, Star Woman	9/5	10/14	9	O

[1] Code for source of material; fill in after material arrives.
R = Reserve (on your library's copy)
B = Borrowed from another branch (intrasystem loans)
I = Interlibrary loan
O = Purchase
X = Other (e.g., cancelled, does not exist)

FIGURE 23 Worked Example of Figure 38: Document Delivery Log

picks up the material, usually the branch or circulation desk, *not* the central ILL unit. If, for example, all system ILLs go through a central ILL unit, but getting the material from there to the branch takes another day or two, measuring **Document Delivery** at the central ILL unit would underestimate the time that the branch patron had to wait. At the central library, log requests wherever the patron picks up the materials.

3. Mark each request in some way (for example, write its request number on it in a distinctive color of ink) so that when the material arrives, you know to update the Document Delivery Log.

  a. In a multi-branch system, each unit or branch should track requests.
  b. Library-level results requires a minimum of 400 requests, distributed among the branches in proportion to their circulation and/or their volume of requests. (The eas-

iest approach is to have each branch track all its requests for a month, then add together the results for all the branches.)

4. Note on the log the source for each item as soon as it is known. With some items, that may be when the request is filled, with others it may be as soon as the request is placed.
5. As the items arrive, note on the log the source of the material (if necessary) and the date on which each becomes available for pickup (*not* the date on which the user did pick it up).

  a. Count the actual days (including days the library was closed) between the date requested and the date available. Do not count the date of the request, but do count the date the item was finally available.

6. Use the Document Delivery Tally Sheet, Figure 39, to calculate the **Document Delivery** figures. (Figure 24 is a filled in example.)

Library __Main__

Date __Sept. 1986__

No. of requests __118__

Availability		Source of Material					
		Reserves	Interlibrary loans	Intrasystem loans	Purchases	Other	ALL
0–7 days	#	3	1	25	0		29
	%	11	2	49	0		24
8–14 days	#	7	4	12			24
	%	27	10	24	50		20
15–30 days	#	12	17	10			39
	%	46	44	20			33
More than 30 days	#	4	17	4	1		26
	%	15	44	7	50		22
Total[1]	#	26	39	51	2		118
	%	99%	100%	100%	100%		99%

[1] Totals may actually be a little more or less than 100% due to rounding.

FIGURE 24 Worked Example of Figure 39: Document Delivery Tally Sheet

Calculate the percent of each type of request available within 7, 14, and 30 days, and more than 30 days, and those cancelled (e.g., the user is no longer interested, the item does not exist, etc.) and those that never arrive.

Example: An item was requested on November 26 and the item was available on December 4. The Document Delivery Time was eight days.

Pointers/Special Considerations

• In some cases, a Document Delivery Log may not be practical, for example, where requests can go in many different directions and there is no convenient central place through which requests are processed. An alternative is to keep the needed information on each request form. For example, during the data collection every request slip may have the originating date written in a distinctive color ink. This would be the signal that when the item is available the date and source of material should be recorded and the request slip put aside to be counted. At some later time someone collects all the slips and fills out Figure 38, Document Delivery Log.

• One caution about labelling the requests this way (or in an even more obvious way, like specially colored paper) is that it signals the staff that this request is being tracked. This could inadvertently result in special treatment. If the sample requests are given priority, the results will not be representative of the library's usual service. The advantage is that in some cases this will be easier than maintaining the log.

• The tracking ends when the item is available, not when the patron picks it up, because patron delays in coming to get it are not within the library's control. However, if you think that the library may contribute to patron delays (e.g., by inconvenient hours), you can easily add to Figure 38 the pick-up date and analyze those delays.

Further Possibilities

• Calculate separate figures for different kinds of materials, for example, adults' versus young adults' and children's books versus periodicals.

• Determine **Document Delivery** for different sources, for example, within-state versus out-of-state interlibrary loans.

Reference Services

Reference service helps the client use information resources inside and outside the library, and provides personalized answers to questions. Two measures apply to reference services:

• **Reference Transactions per Capita**
• **Reference Completion Rate**

Both measures reflect only requests for which people asked the staff for assistance. They do not reflect reference questions that users answer for themselves using the library's resources without staff help.

These measures may be used together or separately. Figure 40 collects the data for both measures simultaneously. Libraries that use their own methods to count **Reference Transactions per Capita** (instead of Figure 40) may not have the data needed for **Reference Completion Rate**.

A reference transaction is defined as an information contact which involves the knowledge, use, recommendations, interpretation, or instruction in the use of one or more information sources by a member of the library staff. It includes information and referral services. Information sources include printed and non-printed materials, machine-readable data bases, catalogs and other holdings records, and, through communication or referral, other libraries and institutions, and people inside and outside the library. The request may come in person, by phone, or mail, from an adult, young adult, or child.

Reference transactions include:

• Requests for help with the catalog (but not mechanical questions, e.g., how to operate a microfilm catalog)
• Questions of fact (or requests for help in finding facts)
• General requests for help (literature searches, readers' advisory services, etc.)
• Requests for information and referral (e.g., questions about agencies or people in the community who provide specific help and/or services)
• Data base searches.

For example:

- "How can I find out when Andrew Wyeth was born?"
- "Who is the author of *Dinner at the Homesick Restaurant?*"
- "Can you help me locate books on the Russian Revolution?"
- "Is there a recycling center in this town?"

Not included:

- Directional transactions such as "Where are the records?" and "I'm looking for a book with the call number 811.2G." (If the user ends up needing more assistance than simple directions, such a question may become a reference transaction.)
- Questions of rules and policies such as "Are you open until 9:00 tonight?"
- Telephone requests for specific library materials, such as "Do you have Thoreau's *Walden?* Is it in? Will you hold it for me?" These are counted in TITLES SOUGHT for the Materials Availability Measures, discussed earlier in this chapter.

Reference Transactions per Capita

Definition: Number of reference transactions per person in the community served.

Calculation: ANNUAL NUMBER OF REFERENCE TRANSACTIONS divided by POPULATION OF LEGAL SERVICE AREA.

Data Collection: If the library does not already count reference transactions, reference staff tallies questions during a one-week sample period.

The ANNUAL NUMBER OF REFERENCE TRANSACTIONS is the total number of reference questions asked in a year. It may be based on either an actual count or a sample.

Example: A library with an ANNUAL NUMBER OF REFERENCE TRANSACTIONS of 34,948 last year served a population of 58,246. Its **Reference Transactions per Capita** was .6.

A library which continuously counts all its reference transactions (using the definition above) already has ANNUAL NUMBER OF REFERENCE TRANSACTIONS (Data Elements Summary Sheet, Figure 26, item d). For the results to be comparable with other libraries, the count must have been made using the definition above. A library that does not count reference transactions, or one that routinely counts reference transactions but not according to this definition, should collect a one-week sample using this definition.

Analysis and Use of Data

This measure does not reflect how well the questions were answered, only how many were handled.

- A high **Reference Transactions per Capita** reflects fairly heavy reliance on staff assistance. This may mean that the library is difficult to use; that users are comfortable approaching the staff for assistance; or that users have complex information needs best met with professional help.
- A low **Reference Transactions per Capita** with a high **Circulation per Capita** may indicate a library used mostly for borrowing materials.
- Low **Reference Transactions per Capita** and **Circulation per Capita** may mean a low level of overall library use by the community.
- High **Reference Transactions per Capita** and low **Title** and **Subject/Author Fill Rates** may indicate that users are frustrated in finding information and materials.
- High **Reference Transactions per Capita** and low **Reference Completion Rate** may indicate an emphasis on speed and volume rather than thoroughness.
- Low **Reference Transactions per Capita** and high **Reference Completion Rate** may indicate an emphasis on serving a few people well.
- High **Reference Transactions per Capita** and low **Library Visits per Capita** may mean that a large proportion of library users are asking reference questions.

Possible approaches to increasing **Reference Transactions per Capita** include:

- Publicize reference service and the kinds of questions you answer
- Increase the visibility of the reference desk
- Encourage the staff to actively offer to help clients who appear to need assistance
- Add innovative information services, such as information and referral or database searching
- Consider whether the reference staff are available and approachable. You may want to increase staffing, change staffing patterns, or change policies and procedures.

Possible ways of reducing **Reference Transactions per Capita** are:

- Consider whether the library can be made easier for people to use on their own
- Look at the kinds of reference questions received most often for a clue as to how to make users more independent
- Analyze the areas in which the most questions are received to see if the collection in those areas should be enhanced.

Collecting and Analyzing the Data

If a library does not currently count ANNUAL NUMBER OF REFERENCE TRANSACTIONS, or if it uses a different definition of reference transactions from the one above, the data can be collected over a one week sample period. It is easy to count reference transactions for this measure and for **Reference Completion Rate** (discussed later in this chapter) at the same time using Figure 40, the Reference Tally Sheet.

1. Collect the data during a one week "typical" period (see Scheduling in Chapter 2). During that week, all staff who handle reference transactions count each reference transaction as it occurs, wherever it occurs.
2. Count for the *entire week,* not for periods during that week, as is done with the Materials Availability Survey. Reference transactions are fairly easy to count and then the staff don't have to remember to count only part of the day.
3. A common source of confusion is the issue of when a question is a reference question. It's a good idea to start out with a few days' dry run. Let the staff start counting questions, then have a meeting and discuss the kinds of questions that gave them problems. *Then* start counting questions and use the results.

4. Figure 40 is the Reference Tally Sheet you may use to record the number of questions asked and completed. (Figure 25 is a filled in example.)
5. Number all tally sheets before distribution; this way you will know if any sheets are missing.
6. Figure 40 asks you to record questions as completed, redirected, or not completed. This is for the **Reference Completion Rate**. If you are collecting data only for **Reference Transactions per Capita**, not for **Reference Completion Rate**, all you need to count is the number of questions handled, regardless of whether they were answered. See the discussion of **Reference Completion Rate**, below, for details on using Figure 40.
7. Collect the tally sheets at the end of the day or at the end of each person's shift.
8. When the week is over, record totals from all tally sheets. The total number of questions handled is NUMBER OF REFERENCE TRANSACTIONS. Record on Data Elements Summary Sheet, Figure 26, item j.
9. Multiply this total by 52 to get ANNUAL NUMBER OF REFERENCE TRANSACTIONS. Record on Figure 26, Data Elements Summary Sheet, item d.
10. Divide by POPULATION OF LEGAL SERVICE AREA (Data Elements Summary Sheet, item p) to determine **Reference Transactions per Capita**.

Pointers/Special Considerations

- Tally sheets have to be convenient or some questions will not be counted. You might put tally sheets everywhere in the library that they might be needed. Or each staff member may carry around a tally sheet. The tally sheets can be anonymous if the staff are concerned that their personal performance is being evaluated.
- The potential confusion over what to count makes cross-library comparisons less reliable than a within-library comparison over time (where it is more likely that the staff are all counting the same kinds of questions in the same way).
- It is difficult to count questions when the library is at its busiest. The importance of keeping a running tally throughout the day should be stressed with the staff. A sample (counting for a week rather than year-round) may be preferable because it is easier for the staff to be conscientious for a short period. Counting day in and day out all year long may result in the

Library _Main_

Date ___9/15/86___

Time Period _9 am - noon_

A   Reference transactions completed today (user has received requested information on the same day)

	Total
卌 卌 卌 卌 卌 卌 卌 卌 卌I 卌 卌 卌 卌 卌 卌 卌 卌 卌 卌	**95** A

B   Reference transactions redirected (e.g., to another department, another library, or a nonlibrary source)

	Total
卌 卌 卌 卌 卌 卌	**30** B

C   Reference transactions not completed today (includes those completed at a later time)

	Total
卌 卌	**10** C

D   Other questions (includes directional questions and other questions not included in definition of reference transaction, below)

	Total
卌 卌 卌 卌 卌 卌 卌 卌 卌 卌 卌 卌 卌 卌	**70** D

Directions:

1. For each reference transaction, put one hash mark (/) in section A, B, C, or D. Make only one hash mark per transaction.

2. A reference transaction is an information contact which involves the knowledge, use, recommendations, interpretation, or instruction in the use of one or more information sources by a member of the library staff. It includes information and referral services. Information sources include printed and nonprinted materials, machine-readable data bases, catalogs and other holdings, records, other libraries and institutions, and people inside and outside the library. The request may come in person, by phone, or mail, from an adult or a child.

3. For users with multiple questions, record each question as a separate transaction if it deals with a new concern.

FIGURE 25 Worked Example of Figure 40: Reference Tally Sheet

staff estimating "the usual" number of reference questions at the end of a busy day.

•   Branches and multi-branch libraries may find it difficult to determine **Reference Transactions per Capita** if the geographical boundaries of each community cannot be clearly established. (See Population of Legal Service Area, earlier in this chapter.)

Further Possibilities

•   Do separate reference counts for summer and for school year months to provide a more precise ANNUAL NUMBER OF REFERENCE TRANSACTIONS.

•   Tally phone and in-person transactions separately.

•   Develop a more detailed breakdown of reference transactions by type, for example, ready reference versus more complex, and tally questions accordingly. Use whatever breakdown is useful in your library.

- Divide the amount of staff time spent actually answering questions by the number of reference transactions to estimate the average time to answer a question.
- Record questions by time and day, then analyze to determine the times of heaviest workload.
- Record the subjects of questions and determine the most-asked topics.
- Calculate reference transactions per FTE professional staff (or FTE reference staff, or staff time on the reference desk) as an indicator of workload.
- Calculate reference transactions per Hour Open.
- Measure reference transactions separately for children's and young adult services. For example:

  reference transactions answered by the children's services staff and/or using the children's collection.

  reference transactions asked by or on behalf of children.

Reference Completion Rate

Definition: Proportion of reference transactions successfully completed on the same day that the question is asked, in the judgment of the librarian.

Calculation: NUMBER OF REFERENCE TRANSACTIONS COMPLETED divided by NUMBER OF REFERENCE TRANSACTIONS.

Data Collection: Reference staff tallies a sample set of reference transactions.

This measure reflects users' immediate success in getting their questions answered. The reference transaction must be completed *within the same working day* it was initiated to be counted as completed for this measure. In the interest of simplicity, no provision is made for partial completion or for questions that are completed at a later time.

Whether a question is completed is left to the judgment of the staff member. For example, if the library does not have exactly what the client requested but the librarian can offer a substitute, the librarian will have to rely on the client's response to judge whether the substitute was satisfactory and therefore whether the question was completed.

Information and referral requests for which the staff member provided an appropriate referral are considered completed. In essence, the question is considered to have been a request for a referral. On the other hand, questions where the user is referred to another library because the first library cannot answer the question (for example, "I'm sorry, we don't have that, you might try the University Library") are *not* completed.

Example: A library recorded 2,381 REFERENCE TRANSACTIONS in one week. 1,565 were completed on the same day; the rest were redirected, completed at a later time, or not completed. Its **Reference Completion Rate** was 66 percent (1,565 divided by 2,381).

Analysis and Use of Data

This measure is limited to the librarians' estimate of the completion rates. No doubt some questions that the librarian considered completed were not answered completely or accurately, or the answers were not appropriate to the user's needs. This measure may tend to overestimate reference service quality. On the other hand, sometimes staff have higher expectations than do users, so the measure may underestimate service quality.

Possible ways to increase **Reference Completion Rate** include:

- Analyze the components of the reference system (both materials and staffing) to identify problem areas
- Ask the reference librarians what kinds of questions are most troublesome and consider

ways to improve the library's capability in those areas
- Encourage reference staff development.

Possible ways to decrease **Reference Completion Rate** are:

- Consider whether the staff are redirecting questions when they should. Often a small branch library should have a low **Reference Completion Rate** because many users should be referred to the central library once the branch's resources have been exhausted.

Collecting the Data

Like the Materials Availability Measures, **Reference Completion Rate** requires a sample size that depends on the confidence interval needed (see Sampling, under Data Collection, in Chapter 3). If you do not wish to calculate your own sample size, you can use the guideline of a preferable 400 requests, but no fewer than 100. However, **Reference Completion Rate** is most easily collected at the same time as **Reference Transactions per Capita**, which requires a sample of one week's worth of reference transactions. Therefore, the following guidelines will help you decide your sample size:

1. If you are collecting data for both **Reference Completion Rate** and **Reference Transactions per Capita** at the same time, record reference transactions, using Figure 40, for at least one week. (Figure 25 is a worked example.) If at the end of one week you do not have at least 100 reference transactions, continue for another week. If after two weeks you still do not have 100 reference transactions, **Reference Completion Rate** is probably not a useful measure for your library.
2. If you are collecting data for **Reference Completion Rate** only, either calculate your own sample size (using "Sampling" section in Chapter 3) or use the rule of thumb of 400 transactions (or, if that is not possible, 100 transactions).

The following discussion assumes that most libraries will collect data for both Reference Measures at the same time.

1. During a one week sample period, have the staff record all reference transactions on the Reference Tally Sheet, Figure 40. See Scheduling in Chapter 2 on how to choose the period. During that week, all staff should count each reference transaction as it occurs,

wherever it occurs. See "Collecting the Data" under the discussion of **Reference Transactions per Capita**, above.
2. Use Figure 40, Reference Tally Sheet, to record the number of questions asked and completed.
3. Number all tally sheets before distribution; this way you will know if any sheets are missing.
4. Reference transactions are recorded as completed, redirected, or not completed.

   a. A reference transaction is complete (Section A on the Reference Tally Sheet) when the librarian judges that the user has received the information requested by the end of the day. An information and referral question for which an appropriate referral is provided is counted as completed.

   b. A question may be redirected (Section B) to another department within the library, to another library, or to an agency outside the library. For example, a branch library might redirect a question to the central library because the branch does not have the appropriate resources. Information and referral questions for which the user has been referred to the appropriate source are completed, not redirected.

   c. Transactions may be not completed for a number of reasons: all such questions are counted in Section C.

   d. If you wish, you may subdivide Sections B and C according to categories that make sense for your library: for example, a question may be redirected within the library, to another library, or to a nonlibrary outside resource.

   e. Section D may be used to record questions that you may count locally as reference transactions but which do not fit the definition used in this manual, for example, directional questions. This gives the staff a place to count such questions and allows you to continue to count questions according to your local definition during the sampling period.

5. Collect the tally sheets at the end of the day or at the end of each person's shift.
6. When the week is over, record totals from all tally sheets.

   a. Add the totals from section A from all Tally Sheets. This is NUMBER OF REFERENCE TRANSACTIONS COMPLETED. Record on Data Elements Summary Sheet, item k.

b. Add the totals from section B.

c. Add the totals from section C on each Tally Sheet.

d. Add the totals from Section A + section B + section C to obtain NUMBER OF REFERENCE TRANSACTIONS. Record on Data Elements Summary Sheet, item j.

7. Divide NUMBER OF REFERENCE TRANSACTIONS COMPLETED by NUMBER OF REFERENCE TRANSACTIONS to get **Reference Completion Rate**.

8. If the NUMBER OF REFERENCE TRANSACTIONS is 600 or less, use Figure 6 to calculate the range for your estimate. Like the Materials Availability Measures, **Reference Completion Rate** is an estimate subject to some uncertainty. See Confidence Intervals in the section on Sampling, under Data Collection in Chapter 3. If your NUMBER OF REFERENCE TRANSACTIONS is 600 or greater, you do not need to calculate a confidence interval because it will be very small.

Further Possibilities

• Measure user perceptions of whether or not the transaction was completed. This requires surveying users as they leave. These will generally differ from librarian perceptions, but a large difference is a cause for concern.

• Determine percentage of transactions completed accurately. Either review the handling of a sample of actual transactions or use proxies to ask questions for which answers are known. See Thomas Childers, "The Test of Reference," *Library Journal* 105 (April 15, 1980): 924–28, or Peter Hernon and Charles McClure, *Unobtrusive Testing and Library Reference Services* (New York: Ablex, 1987).

• Compare department/branch **Reference Completion Rates**. This requires a minimum of 100 (preferably 400) reference transactions from each unit.

• Measure separate **Reference Completion Rates** for children's and young adult services. For example:

Reference Completion Rate for questions answered by the children's services staff and/or using the children's collection.

Reference Completion Rate for questions asked by or on behalf of children. See Douglas L. Zweizig and others, *Output Measures for Children's Services in Wisconsin Public Libraries: A Pilot Project 1984–5* (Madison: Wisconsin Division for Library Services, 1985; ERIC #ED 275 324).

Pointers/Special Considerations

This measure represents the percentage of transactions that were completed on the day they were initiated. Smaller libraries and bookmobiles often serve as reference access points and may have a lower completion rate because they redirect a large proportion of transactions, or get the answer to the user much later. Because reference system designs vary, it will be much more meaningful for a library to look at its own rates over time than to compare itself to others.

Programming

Libraries provide programs to inform, educate, and entertain their clients, and to promote further library use.

• **Program Attendance per Capita** is the annual number of people attending programs per person in the area served.

Program Attendance per Capita

Definition: Program attendance per person in the population served.

Calculation: ANNUAL PROGRAM ATTENDANCE divided by the POPULATION OF LEGAL SERVICE AREA.

Data Collection: Count the audience at all programs during the entire year.

A program is any planned event which introduces those attending to any of the broad range of library services or activities, or which directly provides information through the presentation of talks, films, dramas, etc. Programs need not take place in the library, but the library must be the primary contributor of time, money, or people in the planning or presentation.

Book talks, tours, and film programs at the library are all examples of library programs. A presentation to a class in the public school and a film shown for a service club meeting should also be counted. However, activities such as ongoing exhibits, contests run by the library, handouts, parades, or library booths at fairs would not be considered "programs" for this measure. Use of the library meeting room by groups other than the library itself is not counted, either.

Analysis and Use of Data

Program Attendance per Capita measures use of library services not captured by other measures. For example, some libraries rely heavily on programming to attract certain user groups; this measure reflects that activity.

Possible approaches to increasing **Program Attendance per Capita** include:

- Have more programs
- Publicize programs more
- Involve community members in program planning
- Broaden the types of programs offered
- Repeat successful programs, perhaps at different branches.

Collecting the Data

Use an actual count to determine ANNUAL PROGRAM ATTENDANCE, not a sample, since programming varies over time. If you do not currently keep such a count, you should begin keeping one now and wait to determine this output measure until a year has passed. You may use the Program Attendance Log, Figure 41. Enter the ANNUAL PROGRAM ATTENDANCE on Figure 26, the Data Elements Summary Sheet, item e.

Example: A library serves a jurisdiction with a population of 12,496. The ANNUAL PROGRAM ATTENDANCE is 1,028. 1,028 divided by 12,496 = .08 **Program Attendance per Capita**.

Further Possibilities

- Determine average attendance per program.
- Analyze attendance by type of program—story hours, book talks, films, etc.
- Determine time spent by staff in program preparation and calculate program attendance per staff hour.
- Determine percentage of program attendance accounted for by out-of-library programs.
- Determine attendance at children's programs per child in the community, attendance at young adult programs per young adult in the community, and attendance at adult programs per adult in the community.
- Count ANNUAL PROGRAM ATTENDANCE at programs for children and programs for adults separately; and count ANNUAL PROGRAM ATTENDANCE by children and by adults separately (not everyone who attends a children's program is a child).
- Ask program attendees whether they are regular library users, or came specifically to attend this program.

Appendix
Blank Forms

FIGURE 26 Data Elements Summary Sheet

Library _____

Date _____

Data Element	Your Number	Used in These Measures
a. Annual Circulation		Circulation per Capita Turnover Rate
b. Annual In-Library Materials Use		In-Library Materials Use per Capita
c. Annual Number of Library Visits		Library Visits per Capita
d. Annual Number of Reference Transactions		Reference Transactions per Capita
e. Annual Program Attendance		Program Attendance per Capita
f. Holdings		Turnover Rate
g. Library Registrations		Registrations as a Percentage of the Population
h. Number of Browsers		Browsers' Fill Rate
i. Number of Browsers Finding Something		Browsers' Fill Rate
j. Number of Reference Transactions		Reference Completion Rate
k. Number of Reference Transactions Completed		Reference Completion Rate
l. Number of Subjects and Authors Found		Subject and Author Fill Rate
m. Number of Subjects and Authors Sought		Subject and Author Fill Rate
n. Number of Titles Found		Title Fill Rate
o. Number of Titles Sought		Title Fill Rate
p. Population of Legal Service Area		Circulation per Capita In-Library Materials Use per Capita Library Visits per Capita Program Attendance per Capita Reference Transactions per Capita Registrations as a Percentage of the Population

FIGURE 27 Output Measures Summary Sheet

Library _____

Date _____

Measure	Calculation	Result
Browsers' Fill Rate[1]	Number of Browsers Finding Something (i) divided by Number of Browsers (h)	
Circulation per Capita	Annual Circulation (a) divided by Population of Legal Service Area (p)	
Document Delivery	% of requests filled: within 7 days 8 to 14 days 15 to 30 days more than 30 days	
In-Library Materials Use per Capita	Annual In-Library Materials Use (b) divided by Population of Legal Service Area (p)	
Library Visits per Capita	Annual Number of Library Visits (c) divided by Population of Legal Service Area (p)	
Program Attendance per Capita	Annual Program Attendance (e) divided by Population of Legal Service Area (p)	
Reference Completion Rate[1]	Number of Reference Transactions Completed (k) divided by Number of Reference Transactions (j)	
Reference Transactions per Capita	Annual Number of Reference Transactions (d) divided by Population of Legal Service Area (p)	
Registrations as a Percentage of the Population	Library Registrations (g) divided by Population of Legal Service Area (p)	
Subject and Author Fill Rate[1]	Number of Subjects and Authors Found (l) divided by Number of Subjects and Authors Sought (m)	
Title Fill Rate[1]	Number of Titles Found (n) divided by Number of Titles Sought (o)	
Turnover Rate	Annual Circulation (a) divided by Holdings (f)	

NOTE: Letters in parentheses refer to Figure 26.
[1] Enter lower and upper limits of the confidence interval as well as the actual figure derived from the data.

FIGURE 28 Library Visits Tally Sheet

Date _____

Entrance _____

Use one tally sheet each day. Enter number of hours during which data were collected.

A: Morning visits. Morning is from ____ a.m. to noon, or ____ hours.

Total

B: Afternoon visits. Afternoon is from noon to ____ p.m., or ____ hours.

Total

C: Evening visits. Evening is from ____ to ____ (closing time), or ____ hours.

Total

FIGURE 29   Estimate of Annual Number of Library Visits

1. Total of all weekday morning visits made during the sample periods. (See Library Visits Tally Sheet, Section A)	(1)
2. Number of weekday morning hours in the sample periods. (e.g., 3 hours Monday morning + 3 hours Wednesday morning = 6)	(2)
3. (1) divided by (2) = average number of weekday morning library visits per hour.	(3)
4. Number of weekday morning hours the library is open each week	(4)
5. (4) × (3) = the estimated number of weekday morning visits per week	(5)
6. Repeat steps 1–5 for (a) afternoon, (b) evening, (c) Saturday, and (d) Sunday visits and hours, and record the estimated number of (a) weekday afternoon, (b) weekday evening, (c) Saturday, and (d) Sunday visits per week	(6a) (6b) (6c) (6d)
7. (5) + (6a) + (6b) + (6c) + (6d) = the estimated number of visits each week.	(7)
8. Line (7) × 52 = average number of visits per year	(8)
9. If not counted at the door, record the number of persons attending in-library programs for the entire month during which the door count is taking place and multiply by 12; OR enter annual meeting room use (if known).	(9)
10. If not counted at the door, record the total number of persons using the library meeting room for the entire month during which the door count is taking place, and multiply by 12; OR enter annual meeting room use (if known).	(10)
11. Add (8) + (9) + (10) to obtain the estimated ANNUAL NUMBER OF LIBRARY VISITS. Record on Data Element Summary Sheet, item (d).	(11)
12. Divide (11) by POPULATION OF LEGAL SERVICE AREA (Data Element Summary Sheet, Figure 26) for **Library Visits per Capita**	(12)

NOTE: This method to be used only if one-week sample is not possible. See text, "Approximating This Measure."

FIGURE 30 In-Library Materials Use Log

Library _____

Date _____

Use one tally sheet for each day. Every hour on the hour collect and count the materials left for reshelving. Enter the time at the top of the form.

Type of Material	Hour												Total
Books													
Magazines													
Pamphlet Files													
Sound Recordings													
Newspapers													
Controlled Materials[1]													
Other													
Totals													

[1] Desk reserve or other materials user has to check out for in-library use.

FIGURE 31 Holdings Estimation Worksheet

		Cards per Inch	Vols. per Card
1. Take ten one-inch samples from the shelflist.		1a	b
		2a	b
		3a	b
For each sample count:		4a	b
		5a	b
(a) cards per inch		6a	b
		7a	b
(b) volumes[1] per card		8a	b
		9a	b
		10a	b
2. Average together the ten samples to get: (c) Average Number of Cards per Inch (d) Average Number of Volumes[1] per Card		2c	d
3. Measure the entire shelflist for Total Shelflist Inches.		3	
4. Multiply the Average Number of Cards per Inch (2c) by the Total Shelflist Inches (3) = Estimated Number of Cards in Shelflist.		4	
5. Multiply the Average Number of Volumes per Card (2d) by Estimated Number of Cards in Shelflist (4). Result is Estimated Number of Volumes in Shelflist.		5	
6. Enter number of items for any materials not included in the shelflist.[2]		6	
7. Add (5) + (6) for Total Library HOLDINGS.		7	

[1] For nonprint items, count number of items (i.e., multiple copies). See text.
[2] See definition of HOLDINGS in text.

FIGURE 32 Calculating the Materials Availability Survey Sample

	Your Library	OR	Default[1]
1. Desired number of title requests[2]			400
2. Title requests per questionnaire			.6
3. Target number of questionnaires (line 1 divided by line 2)			670
4. Response rate			.7
5. Number of questionnaires to hand out (line 3 divided by line 4)			960
6. Expected questionnaires distributed per hour[3]			no default value
7. Number of hours to distribute questionnaires (line 5 divided by line 6)			

[1] If data are lacking for an individual library, use these recommendations.

[2] Since most libraries receive fewer title requests than subject or browsing searches, basing the sample size on titles ensures an adequate size for all three.

[3] Use your own library's data on visits, circulation, whatever is available.

FIGURE 33 Materials Availability Survey Form

Form number _____

LIBRARY SURVEY

Library _____   Date _____

PLEASE FILL OUT THIS SURVEY AND RETURN IT AS YOU LEAVE.

We want to know if you find what you look for in our libraries. Please list below what you looked for today. Mark "YES" if you found it, and "NO" if you did not find it.

TITLE

If you are looking for a specific book, record, cassette, newspaper, or issue of a magazine, please write the title below. Include any reserve material picked up.

NAME OF WORK   FOUND?
(Example)
• Gone with the Wind   YES   NO

1. _____

2. _____

3. _____

4. _____

5. _____

SUBJECT OR AUTHOR

If you are looking for materials or information on a particular subject or a special author today, please note each subject or person below.

SUBJECT OR AUTHOR   DID YOU FIND
(Examples)   SOMETHING?
• how to repair a toaster
• any book by John D. MacDonald   YES   NO

1. _____

2. _____

3. _____

4. _____

5. _____

BROWSING   If you were browsing and not looking for anything specific, did you find something of interest?

YES _____   NO _____

OTHER   _____ Check here if your visit today did *not* include any of the above activities. (Example) using the photocopy machine.

COMMENTS   We would appreciate any comments on our service and collections on the back of this sheet.

THANK YOU!

FIGURE 34 Materials Availability Fact Sheet

This survey measures how successfully people find the materials they are looking for in the library.

DIRECTIONS

1. During the survey time periods, *give a form to each person entering the library*. Explain that a survey is being taken today and the user's cooperation is appreciated. An appropriate comment would be "The library is doing a survey today. Please take one of these and fill it out just before you leave. Thank you." Do not ask in a manner that allows a simple "no" answer, such as "Will you please fill out this form today?"

2. Some terms used on the survey form:
   a. A TITLE search is for a specific book for which the user has all or part of the author or the title.
   b. A SUBJECT OR AUTHOR search is one where the user is looking for something (but not a specific item) on a subject, or anything by a certain author.
   c. BROWSING is looking for "something good to read," not something specific. A person can do a subject or title search and browse on the same visit.
   d. Someone who came into the library not to look for materials but *only* to do something else (use the copy machine, use the restroom, return a book, etc.) should check the OTHER question at the bottom.

3. *EVERY person* (adult and child) *able to fill out the survey form, alone or assisted, must be given one.* Adults may fill out forms for children. You should help any users who need assistance.

4. *If a user is looking for too many items to write down,* ask how many subjects he or she was looking for and how many were found (ask the same for titles), and write those numbers on the survey form in the appropriate spaces. For example, if a user is looking for items on a bibliography, count the number of items on the bibliography and enter that number under "Title" on the survey form. Enter the number found under "yes" in the next column.

5. Ask each person to drop his or her form in the collection box.

6. *If a librarian identifies a specific title for a patron* as a result of a patron's question, this is a title search when the patron looks for the title.

7. *Answer questions about the form* but do not influence the responses in any way. The following answers to questions may prove helpful.

SOME STOCK ANSWERS TO QUESTIONS

1. *Why are you surveying me? Why don't you survey someone else?*
   "This survey period has been chosen to ensure that we get a representation of *all* our library users. It's important for the accuracy of the survey that everyone complete the survey form. Your answers are important."

2. *You gave my friend a questionnaire when he came in a little while ago: can I have one too?*
   "Thank you for being willing to help, but we are only surveying people who come into the library during specific time periods. This is to ensure that our findings are statistically correct."

3. *I really don't have time for this today!*
   "The survey only takes 5 minutes. You'll help us a lot if you can give your time, and your information is important to our study." If the respondent insists, mark the form "REFUSED" and put it in the collection box OR tally a refusal, whichever method your library is using.

4. *I already filled out a form the last time I was here.*
   "Thank you, but we do want you to fill out another one today."

5. *Who's doing the study?*
   "The _____ Library is doing this survey. I am a library staff member (or volunteer) helping with the survey."

6. *Do I write down only books, or records and magazines, too?*
   "All kinds of materials are included, not just books."

7. *Should I count materials I looked at in the library but didn't check out?*
   "Yes. This survey measures both things you use here and those you take home."

8. *Should I fill out the form for my children while we use the library today?*
   "Yes. It is important to us to know if they are finding what they want, too."

9. *I just came in to return a film.*
   "Fine, then you only have to check the 'Other' question at the bottom of the form and turn it in as you leave. But if you do end up looking for something else while you are here, please write that down."

FIGURE 35 Telephone Request Tally Form

Library _____

Date _____

Use one tally form for each day

TITLE REQUESTS:

On shelf	Not on shelf
TOTAL:	TOTAL:

SUBJECTS AND AUTHORS REQUESTS:

On shelf	Not on shelf
TOTAL:	TOTAL:

Count all telephone calls asking whether specific materials (specific books, issues of magazines, film titles, etc.) are currently available. Count as "on shelf" materials that you find on the shelf, that the user could pick up immediately. Count as "not on shelf" materials that are not owned, on order, out in circulation, or otherwise currently unavailable.

FIGURE 36 Materials Availability Survey Tabulation Form

Form Number	(1) Title		(2) Subject/Author		(3) Browsing		(4) Other	
	(a) Number Sought	(b) Number Found	(a) Number Sought	(b) Number Found	(a) Browsers	(b) Found Something	(a) Other	(b) Refused, Blank, or Missing
TOTAL								
Enter on Figure 37	line 7	line 10	line 13	line 16	line 19	line 20	line 3	line 5
	TITLES SOUGHT	TITLES FOUND	SUBJECTS/ AUTHORS SOUGHT	SUBJECTS/ AUTHORS FOUND	NUMBER OF BROWSERS	BROWSERS FINDING SOME-THING	OTHER	NOT USABLE

FIGURE 37 Materials Availability Survey Summary

Response Rate	
1. Number of questionnaires handed out	
2. Questionnaires returned with usable title, subject and author, or browsing answers (total questionnaires minus the total of columns 4a and 4b, Figure 36)	
3. Questionnaires with *only* "Other" question checked (total of column 4a, Figure 36)	
4. Usable questionnaires (subtotal lines (2) + (3))	
5. Questionnaires marked "refused," with no usable responses, or never returned (total of column 4b, Figure 36)	
6. Response rate (line (4) divided by line (1))	

Title Fill Rate	
7. TITLES SOUGHT (total of column 1a, Figure 36)	
8. Titles not available (Telephone Request Tally Form, Figure 35)	
9. Total TITLES SOUGHT (line (7) + line (8))	
10. TITLES FOUND (total of column 1b, Figure 36)	
11. **Title Fill Rate** (line (10) divided by line (9))	
12. Confidence interval for **Title Fill Rate** (See Figure 6)	LOW:
	HIGH:

FIGURE 37 Materials Availability Survey Summary (continued)

Subject Fill Rate	
13. SUBJECTS AND AUTHORS SOUGHT (total of column, 2a, Figure 36)	
14. Subjects and Authors not available (Telephone Request Tally Form, Figure 35)	
15. Total SUBJECTS AND AUTHORS SOUGHT (line (13) + line (14))	
16. SUBJECTS AND AUTHORS FOUND (total of column 2b, Figure 36)	
17. **Subject and Author Fill Rate** (line (16) divided by line (15))	
18. Confidence interval for **Subject and Author Fill Rate** (see Figure 6)	LOW:
	HIGH:

Browsers' Fill Rate	
19. NUMBER OF BROWSERS (total of column 3a, Figure 36)	
20. NUMBER OF BROWSERS FINDING SOMETHING (total of column 3b, Figure 36)	
21. **Browsers' Fill Rate** (line (20) divided by line (19))	
22. Confidence interval for **Browsers' Fill Rate** (see Figure 6)	LOW:
	HIGH:

FIGURE 38   Document Delivery Log

Library _____

Date Begun _____

Date Ended _____

Request No.	ID for Item	Date Requested Month/Day	Date Available Month/Day	Response Time (days)	Code[1]

[1] Code for source of material; fill in after material arrives.
R = Reserve (on your library's copy)
B = Borrowed from another branch (intrasystem loans)
 I = Interlibrary loan
O = Purchase
X = Other (e.g., cancelled, does not exist)

FIGURE 39 Document Delivery Tally Sheet

| | | Library _____ |
| Date _____ |

No. of requests _____

Availability		Source of Material					
		Reserves	Interlibrary loans	Intrasystem loans	Purchases	Other	ALL
0–7 days	#						
	%						
8–14 days	#						
	%						
15–30 days	#						
	%						
More than 30 days	#						
	%						
Total[1]	#						
	%						

[1] Totals may actually be a little more or less than 100% due to rounding.

FIGURE 40 Reference Tally Sheet

Library _____

Date _____

Time Period _____

A   Reference transactions completed today (user has received requested information on the same day)

	Total
	A

B   Reference transactions redirected (e.g., to another department, another library, or a nonlibrary source)

	Total
	B

C   Reference transactions not completed today (includes those completed at a later time)

	Total
	C

D   Other questions (includes directional questions and other questions not included in definition of reference transaction, below)

	Total
	D

Directions:

1. For each reference transaction, put one hash mark (/) in section A, B, C, or D. Make only one hash mark per transaction.

2. A reference transaction is an information contact which involves the knowledge, use, recommendations, interpretation, or instruction in the use of one or more information sources by a member of the library staff. It includes information and referral services. Information sources include printed and nonprinted materials, machine-readable data bases, catalogs and other holdings, records, other libraries and institutions, and people inside and outside the library. The request may come in person, by phone, or mail, from an adult or a child.

3. For users with multiple questions, record each question as a separate transaction if it deals with a new concern.

FIGURE 41 Program Attendance Log

Library _____

Month _____

Date	Name of Program	Number Attending
	TOTAL	

Glossary

Browsers' Fill Rate

Definition: Proportion of browsing searches that are successful.

Calculation: NUMBER OF BROWSERS FINDING SOMETHING divided by NUMBER OF BROWSERS.

Data Collection: Materials Availability Survey, a survey of library users.

CIRCULATION: The total circulation of all materials of all formats that are charged out for use outside the library, including renewals.

Circulation per Capita

Definition: Average annual circulation per person in the community served.

Calculation: ANNUAL CIRCULATION divided by POPULATION OF LEGAL SERVICE AREA.

Data Collection: Most libraries already count circulation.

Document Delivery

Definition: Percent of requests available within 7, 14, and 30 days or longer.

Data Collection: Track one month's worth of requests for up to 30 days.

HOLDINGS: number of cataloged books plus paperbacks and videocassettes, even if uncataloged. Do not include periodicals, even if cataloged. Count volumes or physical items, not titles.

In-Library Materials Use per Capita

Definition: Number of materials used in the library per person served.

Calculation: ANNUAL IN-LIBRARY MATERIALS USE divided by POPULATION OF LEGAL SERVICE AREA.

Data Collection: Ask users not to reshelve, and for one week count all materials used.

Library Visits per Capita

Definition: Number of library visits during the year per person in the community served.

Calculation: ANNUAL NUMBER OF LIBRARY VISITS divided by POPULATION OF LEGAL SERVICE AREA.

Data Collection: Turnstile counter, or count people entering the building during one week.

POPULATION OF LEGAL SERVICE AREA: Number of people in the geographical area for which a public library has been established to offer services and from which (or on behalf of which) the library derives income, plus any area served under contract for which this library is the primary service provider.

Program Attendance per Capita

Definition: Program attendance per person in the population served.

Calculation: ANNUAL PROGRAM ATTENDANCE divided by the POPULATION OF LEGAL SERVICE AREA.

Data Collection: Count the audience at all programs during the entire year.

Reference Completion Rate

Definition: Proportion of reference transactions successfully completed, in judgment of librarian.

Calculation: NUMBER OF REFERENCE TRANSACTIONS COMPLETED divided by NUMBER OF REFERENCE TRANSACTIONS.

Data Collection: Reference staff tallies sample of reference transactions.

Reference transaction: Information contact which involves the knowledge, use, recommendations, interpretation, or instruction in the use of one or more information sources by a member of the library staff. It includes information and referral services. Information sources include printed and nonprinted materials, machine-readable data bases, catalogs and other holdings records, and, through communication or referral, other libraries and institutions, and people inside and outside the library. The request may come in person, by phone, or by mail, from an adult or a child.

Reference Transactions per Capita

Definition: Number of reference transactions per person in the community served.

Calculation: ANNUAL NUMBER OF REFERENCE TRANSACTIONS divided by POPULATION OF LEGAL SERVICE AREA.

Data Collection: If the library does not already count reference transactions, reference staff tallies questions during a one-week sample period.

Registrations as a Percentage of the Population

Definition: Proportion of the people in the community served who have registered as library users.

Calculation: LIBRARY REGISTRATIONS divided by POPULATION OF LEGAL SERVICE AREA.

Data Collection: Count number of registrations in library registration file.

Subject and Author Fill Rate

Definition: Proportion of subject and author searches that are successful.

Calculation: NUMBER OF SUBJECTS AND AUTHORS FOUND divided by NUMBER OF SUBJECTS AND AUTHORS SOUGHT.

Data Collection: Materials Availability Survey, a survey of library users.

Title Fill Rate

Definition: Proportion of title searches that are successful.

Calculation: NUMBER OF TITLES FOUND divided by NUMBER OF TITLES SOUGHT.

Data Collection: Materials Availability Survey, a survey of library users.

Turnover Rate

Definition: Average circulation per volume owned.

Calculation: ANNUAL CIRCULATION divided by the library's HOLDINGS.

Data Collection: Use existing data, or estimate collection size by measuring shelflist.

Biographical Information about the Authors

Nancy A. Van House completed her PhD at the School of Library and Information Studies, University of California, Berkeley, where she is currently Associate Professor. Before her appointment at Berkeley she served as Senior Research Associate at King Research, Inc. She is the author of numerous books and articles including *Public Library User Fees* (Westport, Conn.: Greenwood Press, 1983) and co-author (under the name DeWath) of *A Planning Process for Public Libraries* (Chicago: American Library Association, 1980). She is also co-author of *Planning and Role Setting for Public Libraries* (Chicago: American Library Association, 1987). She does research and consulting on library planning and evaluation, the economics of library services, and the library labor market.

Mary Jo Lynch completed her PhD at Rutgers University. Since 1978 she has held the position of Director of the Office for Research at the American Library Association. She has worked as a reference librarian in academic libraries, has taught in three different library education programs, and has been a frequent contributor to the professional literature. She served as Project Coordinator for the work that led to publication of *A Planning Process for Public Libraries* (Chicago: American Library Association, 1980), and also served on the Steering Committee that guided the development of the first edition of *Output Measures for Public Libraries* (Chicago: American Library Association, 1982). She has completed several projects in the area of library statistics under contract to the U.S. Department of Education. Most recently she directed a pilot project to coordinate data collection done in the state library agencies and served as co-author for *Planning and Role Setting for Public Libraries* (Chicago: American Library Association, 1987).

Charles R. McClure completed his PhD at Rutgers University. He is President of Information Management Consultant Services, Inc., and Professor at the School of Information Studies, Syracuse University, Syracuse, N.Y. He has served as principal investigator on a number of funded projects, including the Public Library Development Project, and works as a management consultant to public, academic, corporate, and state libraries. He is the author or co-author of: *Planning for Library Services* (New York: Haworth Press, 1982); *Strategies for Library Administration* (Littleton, Colo.: Libraries Unlimited, 1982); *Research for Decision Making* (Chicago: American Library Association, 1984); *Planning and Role Setting for Public Libraries* (Chicago: American Library Association, 1987); and a number of other articles and monographs.

Douglas L. Zweizig completed his PhD at Syracuse University. Currently he is Professor at the School of Library and Information Studies, University of Wisconsin–Madison. He previously held the position of Senior Research Associate at King Research, Inc. He has written numerous articles related to planning and performance measures. He is co-author of *Planning and Role Setting for Public Libraries* (Chicago: American Library Association, 1987) and the first edition of *Output Measures for Public Libraries* (Chicago: American Library Association, 1982). He has been a consultant to various libraries and most recently, with Karen Krueger, has completed the report *Standards for Public Library Services in Ohio* (Columbus: State Library of Ohio, 1986).

Eleanor Jo Rodger received her MLS from the University of Maryland. She is currently Executive Director of the Public Library Association. Her previous positions include Chief of State Network Services at the Enoch Pratt Library and Coordinator of Evaluation and Information Development for the Fairfax County (Virginia) Public Library. She is co-author of the first edition of *Output Measures for Public Libraries* (Chicago: American Library Association, 1982) and consults on planning and measurement.

Index

Prepared by Answers Unlimited, Inc.